The White Rose of Truth;

A Mother's Story of Love, Loss

and Justice

Erin White

The White Rose of Truth;
A Mother's Story of Love, Loss and Justice

Copyright © 2011 by Erin White

Thewhiteroseoftruth@gmail.com

Cover design by: Debra Brancato and Erin White
Cover photograph by: Debra Brancato

*To all of you
who knew and loved
Brandon ("Whitey").*

*"In everyone's life, at some time
our inner fire goes out.
It is then burst into flame by an encounter
with another human being.
We should all be thankful for those people
who rekindle the inner spirit."*

~Albert Schweitzer

Acknowledgements

I would first like to thank Riley, Sean and Colleen for putting up with my countless hours at the computer and for allowing me to share their experiences no matter how painful and personal. Thank you to both of our families whose unending support held me up with gentle hands on the darkest days. To the bouncers and all of Brandon's friends. You taught me about love, loyalty and friendship, sharing with me, over countless hours, the Brandon you knew. To Brahim Baytieh, thank you for your tireless quest for justice, your friendship and for being the inspiration of my book title. To Joe Gaul and the many others who worked so very hard for Brandon before and during the trial. Joe, I am thankful for your friendship and am better for knowing you.

To Terri, for her endless support, her editing and encouraging me to, "just write." To Coach Kauo for taking time out of an already busy teaching and coaching schedule to proofread my manuscript. To Debra (Deb) Brancato for "just getting me" and getting me and getting me! To all my girlfriends, who never seem to tire of lending an ear when I need to talk! To my amazing friend Don Moore, without whom, my book would never have become a printed publication. Thanks to my mom for just being my mom and for all those hours at the dining room table when I was a young girl, pushing me to "always write a rough draft first."

I would also like to mention author Dominick Dunne. He too lost a child to violence and even though he was losing his battle with cancer, took the time to write back to me and encouraged me to seek publication.

To my friend Joe and once more to Colleen, special thanks for never losing patience with my unending questions and for your willingness to help me out of technical jams. I cannot forget to thank Google and Thesaurus.com. Both of these reference sites were invaluable during all my hours of researching the rules of book writing, submission and publication.

To Deb (again) for her friendship, her amazing artistry on the cover of this book and her patience! To Joshua and eBook Architects for the formatting help and finally, thank you to all the ebook sites for their author support.

Contents

Preface

For any parent the loss of a child is impossible to fathom. How can one even perceive the thought? Brandon was taken from us in a tragic, painful and unnecessary way. Just as his dreams and goals were beginning to take shape, he was murdered senselessly. He was only twenty-one years old, with his whole life ahead of him.

Originally I just wanted to write an article to share our experiences and to tell Brandon's story, but as I wrote the words kept coming. Soon I had pages and pages and just kept going. I wanted to touch anyone reading my book the same way our family had been touched by the love of so many.

My decision early on was not to use the names of the two men responsible for our family's nightmare. I did not feel they deserved to be named. I began by calling them Defendant 1 and Defendant 2. However, as I continued to write I decided to include actual emails sent to family and friends. What better way, I thought, to journal what really happened? These emails initially updated those closest to us with the progress being made towards the start of the trial. I then wrote nightly emails during the trial for those who could not attend but wanted to be kept up to date.

For this reason, and to preserve the integrity of my emails (I would not have called them Defendant 1 and Defendant 2 in personal emails to family), I have used only the last names of the two men. Those involved with the defendants in any way were also referred to by last name only. In actuality, the name of anyone called to testify in court is considered public record, but I chose not to use his or her full names even though I could have.

As far as our family and friends, I personally asked each and every one mentioned for permission to use their first name. No one declined my request and for that I am grateful. I felt it was important for me to explain ahead of time my decision regarding the use of names.

I have been a little afraid of "being done" with my story. I strove to be accurate and truthful as I wrote of our family's saga but my book is so full of raw emotion I was almost apprehensive at the thought of having others read about it.

The "book" of our family's anguish may never be done. The pain of our loss softens at times but does not diminish. Our love for Brandon never wavers.

My words are from the heart, the broken heart of a mother who has suffered the worst kind of pain.

"How can a mother be asked to bury her son?" These are the words I spoke at the sentencing of the two men responsible for the death of my son.

Brandon, with his gorgeous red hair and beautiful smile was just 21 when he was murdered while helping defuse a fight at a popular sports bar called the Time Out Tavern in Orange County, California, on New Years Day, 2007. This is his story and the story of a path our family, through no choice of our own, was forced to take.

"B" is For Brandon

In the early morning hours of January 1st, 2007, my son died and two others were injured. This was the beginning of a parent's worst nightmare, a phone call in the middle of the night that changed our family, our friends and anyone who knew Brandon, forever.

Brandon, Bran, Whitey, "B", all endearments for a man described by many as a gentle giant. At a height of 6'3", he towered over me but was so kind in spirit and the most loving and caring son a mother could ask for.

Born on May 4th, 1985, Brandon was the middle of our three children. He arrived at 5:03 a.m. at Mission Community Hospital in Mission Viejo, California. He drew his first breath in that hospital and was pronounced dead at 2:30 a.m. in the same hospital, just five months shy of his twenty-second birthday.

I used to tease him about being the hardest of the three to deliver. The way he was positioned in my pelvis made his birth the most difficult I would have. During his delivery, Dr. May motioned to my husband and said, "Hey Riley, come look, I think the baby will have red hair just like his brother Sean." It was true! I delivered a healthy boy and another red head! I will be honest, I had dreamt of pink bows and frilly dresses and baby girls with this pregnancy. Ultrasound was not commonly done in uncomplicated pregnancies in the mid 80's, so we had no idea what sex our child would be. However, when Dr. May said, "Sean has a baby brother" and Brandon was put in my arms for the first time, all other thoughts were forgotten and the love poured from me into my beautiful boy.

Brandon was a really good baby. I always thought that it might be because Riley and I were calmer and more confident with the second baby. We had already been through everything once and mostly knew what to expect and what to do. He was just a very mellow kid all around. He slept well, ate well, and loved his momma! He had a ready smile and didn't cry a lot. He and older brother Sean were two years and nine months apart. They were good company for each other and were always very close right from the start.

We still could not believe we had not one but two red headed kids. My immediate family has no red heads (although my mother swears there are red headed cousins somewhere). Riley's beard was reddish (when we first met) although his hair was more of a dirty blond in color. Riley's younger sister Peggy has red hair and his mom was red haired in her younger days, so I always figured that's where the red hair came from.

How do you begin to sum up your child in a few paragraphs? I believe any parent could write a novel when it comes to describing their children. They are all different, unique and so special.

Brandon (I called him Bran most of the time) had hazel eyes like mine. While mine can look green occasionally, Brandon's were more on the brown side. He had a birthmark on the inside of his left ankle. It was about two inches around and looked just like the batman symbol from the TV show and the movies. We used to tease him about it. The teasing never seemed to bother him. I think he thought the birthmark was cool.

While Sean was a thumb sucker as a baby, Brandon loved his pacifier. Heaven forbid we did not have a back up close by if one fell behind the crib. When he was old enough to understand, I'd say around age two, I secretly cut the tip of the pacifier off. "Uh oh", I said, "It broke Brandon." He got to throw it away himself. No one took it from him. In his mind he was done with it. I thought I was pretty smart at the time that my "master plan" had worked.

I used to sing to him and Sean before bed. Both the boys loved the song, Inch Worm. As I sang, "Inch worm, inch worm, measuring the Marigolds, seems to me you'd stop and see how beautiful they are", Brandon changed the words at the end and sang, "Seems to me you'd stop and see how beautiful mommy is!" My heart melted. I have never forgotten how very sweet he was and how it warmed my heart when he sang his version of the song to me.

One of my many favorite childhood memories of Brandon was the Christmas we bought him a Little Tykes Cozy Coop. He must have been around three. He LOVED that thing and rode all around in it. It was a bright red car made from that special Little Tykes heavy plastic. It had a rounded top and a bright yellow door you could open to get in and out. Inside there was a steering wheel and a horn. To make it go you had to use your feet. He had such a grin on his face every time he was in it. I am sure if I were able to ask him now he would say that his Cozy Coop was one of his favorite memories, as well. The happiness on his little face is something I will forever remember.

Bran loved to build with Lego's and also Play Mobile figures. Remember, this was the mid to late 1980's and Play Mobile was popular. They were little plastic figures of sailors or truck drivers or firemen etc. You could buy the vehicles and accessories for all the figures. His favorites were the pirates, the pirate ship, the Indians and the teepee. He played with them for hours!

He was a typical boy and loved to get dirty. He swam, rode his bike or his razor scooter and played on the jungle gym the most. I was always so afraid that the boys might fall off the jungle gym; I couldn't watch them on it so Riley had jungle gym duty!

His favorite Disney movie as a child was Lady and the Tramp. He always wanted to watch "Hady Tramp" as he called it. He asked to watch it over and over again. Brandon loved Sesame Street, Mister Roger's Neighborhood, Teenage Mutant Ninja Turtles, and when he got older, The Simpson's and, much to my dismay, that show Jack Ass. He and Sean sat in their room and just laughed and laughed.

Brandon's personality was like his Dads, more quiet and thoughtful. He made friends easily and he always, even from a young age, stuck up for the littler guy. He hated when people were treated unfairly or badly. He had many friends of all races, colors, and creeds.

Brandon's sister, Colleen, was born when he was five and Sean was nine. Bran definitely had "middle child syndrome" and wasn't quite certain about this new baby sister. He wasn't mean or anything but was just not sure he wanted to share mom. Brandon enjoyed playing with Colleen as she lay on the floor on a blanket. He helped me with her when I needed a diaper and such but in his mind I think he felt she got more attention.

In school, Brandon was always one of the tallest in his class. He had his pudgier stage at around ten or eleven and I worried that he would never grow out of it. My mom told me that she didn't think kids grew up and out at the same time and to be patient. She raised six children so I tended to believe her. Turned out, mom was right! He grew to be very tall and weighed about 240 pounds, give or take; depending on what sport he was playing at the time. Brandon wore a size 16 shoes and his voice was deeper like his dads.

He was not the freckly type of red head but had his share of acne as a teen. Being involved in sports with all that sweating did not help. With treatment to get him past the worst, he grew up to be very handsome with smooth unblemished, skin!

The boys played AYSO soccer in their youth, as well as flag football. Both went on to play football in both high school and college. Bran was also on the track team for a season his senior year in high school. He competed in shot put and discus and as a matter of fact, did very well.

Brandon and Sean actually played high school football simultaneously. We were lucky enough to see the boys in a game together. What a wonderful sight to see your sons, side by side, playing a game they loved. Bran loved to play the game but detested the workouts. When he was a sophomore he was given the honor to dress out and be on the field for Varsity while officially on the J.V. team. Sean was a senior on Varsity. It was a proud moment for us as parents to hear the announcer say, "Tackle made by White and White". This was a special memory that Bran and Sean remembered and talked about often.

One of our favorite memories of Brandon is our trip to Las Vegas to celebrate his twenty-first birthday. We started this tradition when Sean turned twenty-one. Bran could invite three friends to share a room with in Vegas. Riley and I put the boys up at one hotel and we, (to save our sanity) stayed at another. We treated him and his friends to one nice meal. It was up to them to get to Vegas and meet the rest of their expenses. It was so cool to teach Brandon to play Blackjack (my personal favorite). At one point, we agreed to meet the boys at the Luxor Hotel. Brandon, his friends, Sean and his friend Brian stopped at Excalibur Hotel where, as you walk through the shops, a hotel employee would try and guess your weight. If he was wrong you got to choose a prize such as a Viking helmet. I will never forget seeing Brandon and Sean walking up the aisle of the Luxor Casino wearing matching Viking helmets with horns on them. Here were these two big guys with matching red hair in those helmets! It was hilarious. A Kodak moment for sure and one we will never forget.

He and Sean shared a room for 18 years. Sean's side of the room was always a mess and Brandon's side was always much cleaner. Since space was limited, we had purchased the boys matching oak twin beds, the type with the drawers underneath to fit their clothes. Our brilliant plan was that someday when they moved out they would have beds to take with them. By the time they moved out they both wanted larger beds. Who could blame them? Their feet hung over those small twin beds and they were "over it"!

They were so close but so different. Sean was always more outgoing and I know Brandon envied Sean's people skills. Sean envied Brandon's size although he was just a couple inches shorter. Sean always felt it was really unfair that Brandon was the younger brother but the bigger of the two. Although shy, Brandon grew to have more confidence and never seemed to lack for female attention!

Brandon was the first to move out at age nineteen. He and his good friend since high school, Steve, had an opportunity to share a place and grabbed it. Not too long after they moved out, Steve snagged a girlfriend so he and Brandon were not roomies for too long. Sean soon flew the coup as well to share an apartment in Irvine with two friends. It was weird to have them gone. After the boys moved out, it took us a week to get all the tape off the walls and the ceiling in their room. There were pictures of beautiful models plastered everywhere. We scraped and scraped, especially the ceiling. There were also many posters of rock bands and Brandon's beloved fighter planes. You could not even see the paint for all the posters that adorned the walls!

Brandon had always been impressed by anything that had to do with the military. His dad was a corpsman in the Navy so that may have been the source. He was also fascinated with Indians (remember the Play Mobile Indians?). He had an arrowhead collection that had been my dad's and two wooden Indian heads, one a male with the headdress and one a female that my dad had carved. Brandon was also very proud of his collection of antique swords. Along with scraping the walls, there were also many nail holes to cover in his room where he had proudly displayed them!

Brandon was such an interesting person and one with varying tastes; the many facets of his personality often pleasantly surprised me. For one thing he LOVED sushi. I am a fish lover but I prefer the cooked kind and was very amazed that he acquired a taste for sushi.

His dad does not care for fish at all. I think one of his friends must have turned him onto it.

Bran also loved his dad's steaks and spare ribs and my special chicken enchiladas, meat loaf and quiche. He loved Samoa's Girl Scout cookies and New Castle was his favorite beer. He put Tabasco on anything he could and loved spicy food (another preference he did not get from me!). Brandon adored chocolate covered cherries and we always got him a box full at Christmas as a special treat.

I would have to say that one of Brandon's great joys was the ocean. He grew up living fairly close to the beach. One of my most favorite pictures is of Brandon and me on the pier in San Clemente. We were waiting to have dinner at the Fisherman's Restaurant and had strolled as a family out onto the pier. We stopped to gaze out over the water and Riley took our picture.

Brandon was so proud of his big black Dodge Ram truck. We were tired of the boy's old cars leaking oil all over our driveway. Getting them each a truck seemed the right thing to do at the time. They were both supposed to help pay each month but I will not get into how that turned out! Those trucks certainly did not seem as huge at the car lot as they were in our driveway! Brandon loved that truck and had one of those noisier mufflers added to it. We always knew when he came around the corner and onto our street. Riley and I would look at each other and say "Brandon's home!" I will say that if

he was late getting home he always made sure to coast around the corner to our house as not to wake the neighborhood. He was just that way, always thinking of others.

Paint balling was a favorite past time of Brandon's. He and a bunch of guys, sometimes including his dad, often traveled down to Camp Pendleton. On one occasion when Riley had tagged along, they played against another group that had shown up that day and it turned out to be the S.W.A.T. team from Santa Ana! How cool was that!

Brandon loved nice clothes. He saved and saved to get what he wanted, but was happiest in his Rainbow sandals and wore them all the time. It was quite a challenge to find shoes in a size 16!

He enjoyed all sorts of music from Metallica to Bocelli. We often found him studying while classical music played on the computer. I was so pleased that he was drawn to many types of music. Sean, Brandon and I shared a love of music. I quizzed them in the car when we were together to see if they could name the song on the radio. It was always a song from a group that I liked and they often knew it! I am happy to say that Colleen also caught the music bug.

He was a positive role model, a wonderful, loving son, and a loyal friend. He touched many with his generosity and his caring. Brandon was such a presence in a room. A ready smile lit up his face and those around him felt its warmth. He was polite and kind and made everyone feel safe. He was the happiest when with his friends, put others before himself and would do anything for anybody. I can't tell you how many times he offered his truck to move friends from one place to another. He never complained about helping a friend. Empting the dishwasher for me, now that was another story!

I feel this chapter would not be complete without the story of "Oi". Brandon and his friends, especially Blake and Steve used this "word" or saying if you will, all of the time. I asked Steve where "Oi" came from. Steve said I really needed to talk to Blake about its origin. Blake had been Bran's friend since high school as well. I remember in their senior year, Brandon used to get up early to stop at Blake's house before school and literally pull Blake out of bed to get ready and then drove him there.

Blake told me that "Oi" was an expression that his family had used for a long time. After high school graduation, the boys, including Steve and Brandon, were at a rented beach house in Newport Beach with Blake's family. While some family members tried to sleep on an upper level, Brandon and the boys were being noisy downstairs. Blake's cousin screamed out the word loudly, according to Blake. Brandon said, "What did you say!" and "Oi" was born. Brandon adopted the term, which can be said loudly or softly, shortened or lengthened out depending on the need at the time.

For example, "OOOOOyyyyeeee", stretched out, could mean they had seen a cute girl. "Oi" could be used to say something was cool, made you mad, happy, exasperated or as Blake demonstrated for me over the phone, as a loud Viking war cry. Blake said Brandon used to "push him to do better" with the Viking war cry on the football field in college.

Brandon always struggled in school but kept on trying, never giving up. He set a goal to attain a college degree in Criminal Justice. He worked his way through community college and into the California State University at Fullerton. He had just finished his first semester there and had all his classes picked out for the next.

Brandon worked two jobs while attending college. His ultimate goal was to be an Orange County Sheriff's Deputy. He wanted to serve and protect. He was actually in the test taking process at the time of his death. We were so proud of him and the fact that he knew what he wanted to do and was working towards it.

Our very good friend Guy, who is a Sergeant with the Orange County Sheriff's Department, was mentoring Brandon. Guy had arranged for Brandon to tour the jail and go on several ride a-longs and gave him advice on what to expect and how to prepare for the tests. Guy felt Brandon would make an excellent addition to his team and looked forward to working with him. Brandon looked up to Guy and respected him so much and with Guy's guidance was motivated to succeed.

While going to school Brandon worked construction by day and at the "Tavern", as they called it, as a bouncer at night. He used to say it was mostly boring at the bar but I always wondered if he said that for my benefit so I wouldn't worry.

The Tavern was not in a bad neighborhood or in a city with a high crime rate. Brandon just worked there for extra money. Most of his coworkers were friends (like Steve) and former high school and college football players also trying to earn extra money. I know he loved the fact that he could work with his friends. Several of the bouncers were also current or former military (Marines and Navy mostly) trying to supplement their incomes.

I told him all the time that I hated him being a bouncer and that some day "someone was going to have a knife". As a parent, I was fearful that someone, some night would do something stupid and Brandon would be hurt. Arguments escalate, tempers flare and tragedies happen. He knew very well how I felt. I knew that the extra money he made there was the motivation for him staying. All the guys he worked with got along so well and I know that was also part of the reason he stayed. I knew the nighttime hours worked with the rest of his busy schedule. I wondered when he ever slept.

He was up by 6 a.m. to work his day job and then go to school. After school, there was homework and then off to the bar. He did not get off until at least 2 a.m. and often waited to make sure the cocktail waitress's got safely to their cars. That left very few hours to rest.

I understood his need for the extra money, but every night I worried about him. I worried something might happen that would be out of his control. He often talked about the "stupid drunk people" that the bouncers had to deal with; patrons who had too much to drink and fought amongst themselves or tried to pick a fight with the bouncers.

I never dreamed that my words and my worst fear would become reality. I guess I told him I was afraid someone would have a knife someday because that was one of the most horrible things I could imagine might happen to him as a bouncer. I guess I was hoping my words might change his mind about that job. He passed off my warnings and said in that deep voice of his, "mom, mom, shh, shh, shh, I need the money".

Brandon by now was sharing a condo with his good friend Josh so he needed to pay rent and expenses. We were helping him out by covering the cost of his classes at school. Brandon and Josh's condo was in Dana Point. He was tired but happy.

Please, Wake Us Up From This Nightmare!

As it happened, several of his friends including Josh, Patrick, Mark and Jerod were heading up to Lake Tahoe for the New Year's holiday. Brandon wanted to go but worried about paying rent and no matter how the boys tried to change his mind, he still felt he could not afford it. He and Josh were planning a trip to New York in February to visit a friend of Josh's and then to Minnesota so Josh could show Brandon where he grew up. Brandon felt he had to choose between trips and decided to save for the trip back East. I know the boys regret not kidnapping Brandon and throwing him in the back of the car. How could they have known what was to happen?

Riley and I had been enjoying New Year's Eve at the home of Guy, his wife Gina and two other couples. Sean, 24 at the time, was at a party and Colleen; age 16 was at a sleepover. We spoke to Brandon, Sean, and Colleen at midnight, like we did every year when we were not all together. It may have been 12:05 a.m. by the time we reached Brandon on his cell phone. I told him I loved him and looked forward to seeing him later in the day and he said he loved me too. He and his dad also spoke briefly.

If anything was going on at the bar during the call you could not tell it from the tone of his voice. I said "Happy New Year" and told him that later, after he slept for a while, he should come on over to watch football and we would have the fixings for sandwiches. I knew he must be busy so we made our call short.

Riley and I came home sometime after 1:30 a.m. and went to bed. At 2:30 a.m. the phone rang, it was one of Brandon's coworkers, Steve (his long time friend and first roommate) saying that Brandon had been hurt and we needed to come. I later found out that Steve had actually told Riley that Brandon had been stabbed in the neck and we needed to go to the hospital. Riley, not wanting to worry me, omitted the stabbing part.

Being a bouncer often meant fending off drunken patrons who were getting out of line and removing them from the bar before they could cause more trouble, hurt others or themselves. Brandon told me once of a patron who threw a beer bottle at the back of his head. Brandon had also been bitten once before as he held a man who was trying to fight with another man. It did not make me feel any better about his job to hear these stories. I will repeat that I hated the fact that he was a bouncer! In the occurrence with the bite, the police became involved and advised Brandon to go the Emergency Room for a tetanus shot. I figured the phone call was regarding something like that since we had gotten a similar late night call after that incident.

Men are quicker dressers; my husband jumped up and was out the door. He was to call me when he found out what was going on. I have often regretted that I did not initially go to the hospital but, being woken up abruptly, I was not thinking clearly and certainly did not know how badly Brandon had been hurt. I know Riley was trying to protect me, but I will always be sorry that I stayed behind.

I did call Sean on his cell phone. I knew he would want to know if he did not already. He was at a party not far from the hospital so said he would meet his dad there. He told me later that as he drove to the hospital he knew in his heart something was wrong. He just felt it.

The minutes seemed like hours as I waited, shaking; holding the phone, hoping Riley would call. What was taking him so long? I became more scared when the phone did not ring. After twenty-five minutes, I could not stand it anymore. I knew the hospital was a twenty minute ride from our home so he had to have gotten there by now. I called his cell phone.

Riley arrived at Mission Community Hospital and there were already many gathered around the E.R. entrance and more arriving. He saw an ambulance in front of the entrance and inside was an Emergency Medical Technician using a bucket to try and clean blood out of the ambulance. Riley remembers seeing a very sad nurse standing there with a mop and a bucket in her hand as well. He says that's when he knew.

Riley ran into the E.R. and up to the reception desk and said, "I need to see my son Brandon!" He was told to have a seat and someone would come out and talk to him. He told me that, surprisingly, the receptionist seemed less than empathetic regarding the urgency in his voice or the reason for him being there. He could not sit so just paced. After about forty-five seconds he said more forcefully, "I need to see someone NOW!"

As he waited, a couple that he did not know came up to him and the woman said how sorry she was. Riley looked at her and said, "Don't tell me that!" He did not want anyone confirming what he feared. A nurse came and asked if he was Brandon's father, he said "yes" and she replied, "Follow me". He was taken into an exam room and was told to wait. A moment later an older doctor, a younger doctor, and a nurse came into the room. Riley told me later that he knew what they were going to say.

The older doctor told Riley that Brandon, while being transported to the hospital, went into cardiac arrest. He ultimately could not be revived and, "had expired". Riley recalls that was the exact word, "expired". He felt the older doctor showed little emotion while giving him such shocking, horrifying news. When Riley was a corpsman (like a medic but with more medical training) in the Navy, he used to have to give devastating information like that to concerned loved ones waiting for news. He remembered thinking that the doctor seemed very lacking in feeling.

Riley remembers pounding his fist onto a mayo tray (a free standing metal tray often in exam rooms used to hold medical supplies and instruments) and then hitting the wall with his fist and saying, "No, No!" The older doctor seemed angry and said, "Call security. I can't have him destroying my exam room." The younger doctor said "No just wait." Riley slumped onto the exam bed that was in the room and remembers thinking that Brandon was the seventh generation of youngest sons and now was gone. He does not know what made him think of that just then.

At this point he heard Sean out in the hall way crying and in unbelievable pain having just heard of Brandon's death. Sean had arrived at the hospital just after Riley and had run up to the desk. As he stood there, Big Joe, a long time friend of Brandon's, took Sean aside and told him of Brandon's murder. That is when Riley heard him cry out. Riley ran out into the hall and wrapped his arms around Sean and tried, unsuccessfully, to console him. This was the very moment he received my call. He saw that it was me calling and vividly remembers thinking that he did not know what he was going to say. How could he possibly tell me?

Riley answered his cell phone and I heard loud wailing in the background. Riley said quietly, and I will never forget his words as long as I live, "He's gone." I said "What?" my voice barely audible and shaky. He said, "He's gone." I could now tell it was Sean crying in the background, "I don't have a brother, they killed my brother, they killed my brother", he cried.

Riley said nothing more so I said I would be right there and hung up the phone. It was almost 3:00 a.m. and I remember standing alone in our room in front of the closet thinking, "I have to get dressed, I have to go!" I didn't know what to put on. I stood there for a long time just staring at the closet, not sure what to do, my mind, blank. It was like my mind could not take it in, could not fathom the thought of what just happened. I was frozen.

Meanwhile, in Tahoe, as all this was happening, Josh and the group with him were ringing in the New Year at a hotel. They decided to get a couple of rooms at that hotel rather than drive back to the cabin they had rented. Josh told me they had only been in their hotel rooms about twenty minutes when he got a phone call on his cell phone from an Orange County Sheriff's deputy. The deputy wanted to know if he had Brandon's parent's phone number. He told the deputy that he didn't have our number with him but would try and get it and call him back. All that the deputy would tell Josh was that Brandon had been cut with a knife and they were trying to locate his parents. Josh immediately called mutual friend Steve's cell and several others. No one was answering their cell phones. Josh found out later that Steve was injured in the incident and could not answer his phone. He called the deputy back and told him he had been unsuccessful in reaching us but that he was Brandon's roommate. Josh said, "You have to tell me what happened!"

The deputy told Josh that Brandon had had his throat cut and was dead. In shock and disbelief, everyone went back to the cabin in Tahoe. By then it was about 3:00 a.m. Grief stricken and crying, they packed up friend Patrick's truck, took turns driving, and headed back to Orange County.

Back at our house I dressed, as if in a trance. I kept repeating to myself "I've got to go; I've got to get dressed." I thought about calling Guy (who would later be really angry at me for not calling) but thought better of it. Guy would surely be asleep and how could I call him at 3 a.m.? I was not thinking clearly. I also briefly considered calling my brother who lived near by but, again, it was the middle of the night and I didn't want to wait for him to come and get me. I just wanted to get to the hospital to be with Riley and Sean. Colleen, at this point, had no idea what had happened. She was most likely asleep.

I drove alone to the hospital hoping the police would magically appear and help me but the streets were deserted at that hour. I am not sure how I got to the hospital. There was not a soul on the streets as I drove. Breathing heavily the whole time, scared and shaking, I was in shock, my mind reeling, trying to wrap my brain around the news. The news was so devastating, I could not think. I could not make myself believe it. It is true what they say about the mind just turning off. I felt my brain was on overload.

As I walked towards the E.R. entrance, there were people everywhere, standing in groups, many were weeping. Someone tall and strong stopped me before I could even get in the door and enveloped me tightly in a hug. I didn't find out until later that it was Ilan, a friend of the boys whom Josh had called. Josh had asked Ilan go to the hospital to offer us support until he could get there.

There must have been 50 or more people outside and inside the E.R. I walked in and saw more people crying. I found Riley and Sean quickly and we were ushered to a tiny room with a few chairs. At the time I thought it odd that we were taken to such a small waiting room.

It was so hot in the room where we were asked to wait. I remember thinking that I couldn't breathe. I must have looked like I was just staring at people. I was overwhelmed with a feeling of "What now?" Out of nervousness Riley and Sean were pacing outside the door, up and down the hall.

There, sitting on the floor, cross-legged, face white as a sheet, was Brandon's girlfriend Regan. We were told that two of Brandon's friends and fellow bouncers Steve and Herb were also hurt. "Oh my God, others were hurt!" I thought. These two boys were two of Brandon's closest friends!

We later wondered how everyone else got to the E.R. before us. We were his family and we were the last ones there! I also wondered why we never got a call from the hospital directly about Brandon. I never did find out why the hospital never tried to contact us but as it turns out, there was a frantic search among Brandon's friends for our home number and Steve was the only one who had it. Brandon's cell phone with all our numbers was in Brandon's pocket.

Riley and I made the decision not to call Colleen. Remember, she was at a sleepover and blissfully ignorant of everything that was happening and nothing would change with her being there. She would be sound asleep. I had to figure out what to say to her. How do I tell her that her brother had been murdered? Sean disagreed with us and felt she should be there but we still decided not to wake her. We argued a bit with him about not calling her. I still think we did the right thing. Sean did not, but he argued no further.

The hospital chaplain came in and tried to talk to us about what would happen next and handed me some sort of pamphlet. She was very nice, but I really didn't want to talk to anyone I didn't know at that moment. She just sat there with us for a while and tried to get us information and told us that two detectives were on the way to talk to us.

Herb's mom, Laura, was there and I remember asking her if Herb was ok. He had a bad injury to his hand that was being tended to. She told me months later that she could not believe I had thought to ask her about her son when we had suffered such a heartbreak. I will never forget the look of pain in her eyes as she recalled that moment when the two of us spoke. I truly believe that in my mind it was easier to ask about Herb and let my mind think of him then to admit why I was really at the hospital.

We were taken to see Steve in a curtained exam room. His jaw had been slashed and had just been stitched up. We were, of course, concerned about him. Anyone who has children knows that your children's closest friends are like your own kids. Not a lot was said by anyone. We were all in distress and I don't think any of us knew what to say. I stood there with my hand on Steve's shoulder. The enormity of what had happened was slowly creeping into my mind. Steve had held Brandon and tried to help him. He had watched his good friend dying.

I have read that when something traumatic happens the mind often tries to blank it out. This was very true for me. It was so surreal to be standing in a hospital in the middle of the night trying to understand that our son had just been murdered. When we were all gathered at Steve's bedside, I felt my mind was a big void and my body was just on autopilot. This wasn't really happening was it? I couldn't feel anything, I couldn't cry. It was a bad dream, right?

As I write this, I wonder how I could even stand up. So many thoughts were going through my head. Surprisingly, during the time at the hospital, I did not think about who had done this to him. It never entered my mind. As I reflect back, you'd think it would be the first thing to ask. I suppose I was just trying to cope with the fact that it had happened at all.

"How did I keep it together?" Why didn't I cry hysterically? Those are questions I have asked myself. I have often thought that, subconsciously, I was denying that it was true, denying that Brandon was truly gone. Where one draws the strength to function at times like this, I cannot say. I think my brain was so numb I couldn't even cry. I must have looked like a deer caught in the headlights.

Two homicide detectives eventually came in to talk to us and I asked immediately to see Brandon. We were told "He was evidence" and that we would not be allowed in the room where he was. I will forever hear those words in my head. I begged one of the detectives to let me go in just for a minute. I promised not to touch anything. He said he was very sorry, but no. I vividly remember asking the detective, "Do you have children?" He said yes, and asked us to please understand they wanted an airtight case. Nothing could be allowed that might contaminate evidence. (As I am proof reading this paragraph, it is painful to relive again the devastation of being denied time with our son.)

While I understood his words, my heart was breaking. I will always regret not just running past them, breaking down the door and going in to my son. This was a homicide; police guarded the door, allowing no one to enter. I would not have been let in, of course, but I still feel it might have made it more real to me to see him. Maybe I should have screamed and wailed.

Riley also regrets not getting to see Brandon. In retrospect, he wishes he had gone directly into the E.R. exam area and not into the waiting area first. Again, it was a matter of not having a clear head and being so distraught and too tired to argue and complain, as we should have.

I still feel it was wrong of them not to let us see him. There has to be a way for a mother and father to be able to see their child after something like this happens. In fact as I write this, I feel the anger rising up in me again at the unfairness of it. Our son was taken from us in a violent way and we were kept from him. The men involved took our son from us and also robbed us of the right to see him. I will never forget that.

In later conversations with our chief investigator, I understood a little better why we were not allowed to see Brandon. I told him how I felt that night about not being allowed to see Brandon. He explained to me that when an investigation begins they do not have all the answers. In fact, mostly just questions at that point. Everything needs to stay airtight so that, down the road, there are no loose ends, no fibers that cannot be accounted for. The logical part of me got that but the emotional mom part of me still wishes we could have had just one minute with him… I know it would have been hard to see him with tubes in this throat where an attempt was made to give him an airway, the blood everywhere, his lifeless body. I don't know how I would have reacted. I have relived that time in the hospital a million times over in my mind.

As a parent, you fear the day that something horrible would ever happen to one of your children. You have nightmares about it. When it actually becomes a reality, you feel powerless. Did he suffer? Was he in pain? What were his last words?

The detectives took all our information and asked questions about Brandon as well. By about 5:00 a.m., the detectives were done with us and there was nothing more to do at the hospital so we came home. Sean went off with some of the guys. I have asked him since about it and he cannot even remember where he went.

Riley and I came home and tried to lie down but could not sleep. How stupid was that, to try and sleep? I think we just didn't know what to do next. We just lay there holding each other. We could not believe what had just gone on. We talked about when to call Colleen.

By 7:00 a.m., I hesitantly called Colleen on her cell phone. I told her we had to pick her up early. We drove the 10-minute drive to her friend Lauren's house and I went to the door. We walked to the car and I got in the back seat with her. She told me later that she thought something had happened to my mom, who is elderly. I told her that Brandon had been killed last night. I felt like I was in a trance and just held her in the back seat while she screamed and screamed, "NO, NO, NO!"

When we got back home, I called Guy. Being a police sergeant, we hoped he might be able to find out some information for us. He was the first person we thought to call. Within minutes Guy and Gina, our friends Denise and Joe, and Liz and Steve, all of whom we had spent the previous evening with, were at our door. After I had called Guy, Gina immediately walked down the street to Liz and Steve's house, sobbing, and told them. They called Denise and Joe. All three couples live in our neighborhood and only had to drive a few blocks. I will NEVER forget their faces as I opened the door. The pain in their eyes spoke volumes and few words were said but I remember the loving hugs.

Guy immediately got on the phone and found out that the police knew who had killed Brandon and were on the way to apprehend the man who had done this awful thing. This just wasn't happening to us, was it?

I then had to start the phone calls. I called my mom next. She was 88 at the time and I worried about calling her. How do you give this information to your child's grandmother? It was so very hard. My mom's voice was catching and as we spoke, she tried to hold herself together. Mom lives with my sister Sheila, and I asked my sister to help call my other family members. Riley called his mom and one of his sisters. I called my supervisor at work, Jenn. I still can't believe I had the where with all to call her. I would certainly not be going into work and needed to tell someone. She had the hard task of calling Dr. May (my long time OB\GYN and my employer), and at my request, a few of my friends and my work partner Terri for me.

In the meantime, it had to have been about 8 a.m. by then; Colleen went across the street to our close friends Deb and Dave's house. When they opened the door, Colleen, crying, fell into the arms of their daughter Chloe. Their son Nico, who had known Brandon all his life cried, when he heard what had happened.

News traveled fast. I work for a large group of physicians and one of the doctors was kind enough to call Dr. Mike Shannon. He had been our pediatrician since Sean was born in 1982, and is also my good friend. He soon arrived at our door just to be there with us. Riley's sister, Cindy arrived with her husband David and their two daughters, Keighley and Chelsea. The cousins are very close. Keighley and Sean are 15 days apart in age and Chelsea and Bran were 12 days apart. Some neighbors soon arrived and while we really didn't feel much like talking, the fact that they were all there to support us was certainly appreciated. We are a very close-knit group and most had known Brandon since he was a little boy. He was three when we moved into our home. There was actually little conversation except for Guy's updates.

My good friend Mariann's eyes still well up with tears when she recalls that she had dressed and was ready to come over, but had been told by Jenn that we really didn't want visitors. I felt so bad about that because Mariann would have been welcome. She told me later how she had wanted to be there for me but thought she was doing what I had requested. I wish I could remember saying I didn't want any company, obviously another example of me not thinking clearly.

Josh and their group got back to Orange County around noon that day. Josh dropped off his things at the condo that he and Brandon shared. He told me it was hard for him walking in since Brandon had just been there with him a few days before. Josh went into his own room to throw his bag down. There, on his bed, was a Christmas gift from Brandon. They had agreed not to exchange gifts so Josh was surprised and sad at seeing the gift. Inside the wrapped package was a painting by the artist Goddard. Goddard is the artist who creates the surrealistic paintings of olives diving into martini glasses, etc, and both he and Brandon loved his work. Josh treasures the painting, which hangs in his home to this day.

How Could This Have Happened?

We found out little by little what had transpired the night before. Four couples went to the Tavern (the bar where Brandon worked) to celebrate New Year's Eve. We were told that the same group had been to the bar a couple of nights before without incident. They had had a good time and decided late on New Year's Eve to go back there to ring in the New Year.

One of the men in the group, Nelson, had been in the Army reserves at one time. We understand he had been released due to his gang related tattoos. Nelson made a deal with an Army recruiter. If he got anyone to sign on, he earned a recruiting commission. He was asking people, including the bouncers, if they were interested in signing up. They weren't interested; in fact, no one Nelson talked to was interested. Nelson became irritating to the patrons. His recruiting efforts were not going well. In addition, he started making disparaging remarks about Marines. The bouncers were concerned that this might cause more problems since there were several Marines in the bar that evening both as patrons and on duty as security. We understand that alcohol was also a factor. For all these reasons, the bouncers decided it was time for Nelson to go.

Nelson was escorted out of the bar. His best friend, Kelley, followed the bouncers as they lead him out. Kelley initially apologized to the bouncers for his friend's actions. Once outside the bar, Nelson started yelling at the bouncers calling them "pussies" and other profane things, over and over again. Kelley joined in and both men removed their shirts to reveal white tank top type undershirts. Nelson realized that some of the people he was trying to recruit were actually Marines. He started to shout out how much better the Army was than the Marines.

The bouncers formed a line in front of the Tavern and told the two friends to "just go home." They even offered to call them cabs, but the aggressiveness continued. It was not uncommon for the bouncers to call a cab for patrons who had too much to drink.

Brandon had several cab companies programmed into the address book of his cell phone so I know that the bouncers did this.

The group of eight friends had arrived in two cars that night, the men all drove in a burgundy Corolla, belonging to Kelley and his girlfriend Ms. Fowler, and the women arrived in a white Saturn driven by Nelson's girlfriend Ms. Barrs. Hank, the head bouncer, stated that he witnessed Kelley going to one of the cars (we believe the white Saturn), open the trunk and appear to take something out and hide it. There was a 911 call from Hank telling the dispatcher that he believed a patron had removed a weapon from the trunk of a car that looked like it might be a gun and to send a patrol car over. We did not find out until much later that Brandon was standing next to Hank when that call was made. Since the sheriff's report was considered evidence, it was not made available to us. We didn't know until the trial where Brandon was at any given moment during the evening. All those months we had no idea if he knew anything about what was going on. I know now that most everything happened after we spoke to him at midnight.

At some point, Nelson's friend Kelley said he was "fed up" and was actually in the burgundy Corolla with one of the men in the group with the last name of Scott. Mr. Scott was behind the wheel and they were in the process of leaving, in fact, they had pulled out of the parking lot when Mr. Scott realized that his girlfriend was still at the bar. Mr. Scott brought the car back around and told Kelley to stay put while got her. Kelley did not wait but got out of the car and went back to the parking lot.

You see, Kelley had more than one opportunity to leave that night but he came back and injected himself back into the situation. Remember, the bouncers had earlier offered to call him a cab. This may be how the premeditation of his actions could be established.

The girlfriends of the two men also tried to get them to leave the bar parking lot. Kelley pushed his girlfriend away and told her to "leave him alone." Ultimately, head bouncer Hank got between Nelson and a small group who were trying to leave the bar. The patrons had to walk past Nelson to get to their car. Nelson initiated a verbal exchange, and we were told a physical confrontation with some in the group trying to leave. We assume Kelley saw this and moved towards his friend Nelson.

Earlier that evening, Brandon's friend Steve, who was not on duty that night, stopped by the Tavern to pick up Brandon's house key.

Steve was to spend the night at Brandon and Josh's condo. Steve said he arrived around 1:00 a.m.

Steve got the key and then Brandon asked Steve to hold his cell phone while he took care of a problem (a broken glass). Steve said "Hi" to a few friends but soon left the bar and was half way to Brandon's condo when he realized he still had Brandon's cell phone. The condo was not far from the bar, so he went back to give Brandon his phone. Steve drove up, realized that there was trouble and at some point met up with Brandon.

Steve and Brandon moved towards Kelley to intercept him. During the trial, the defense claimed that Brandon and Steve attacked Kelley and that Kelley's actions were in self-defense. By his own words, Kelley testified that, "they were heading me off." Brandon may have recognized Kelley as the man seen earlier hiding what he had taken out of the car. They wanted to catch up to him before he got to his friend Nelson and the group of patrons trying to depart.

In addition to yelling at the patrons, Nelson ultimately tried to attack Mr. Ramirez, an active duty Marine who lost his right leg and damaged the other during his service in Iraq. He had served two tours for our country and on his second tour was hit by a rocket-propelled grenade. Mr. Ramirez and his party were just trying to leave when Nelson glanced at Mr. Ramirez' cousin Frankie and demanded, "Bitch, what are you looking at?" Nelson then rushed him and tried to hit him. Mr. Ramirez called to his friend for help. Head bouncer Hank positioned himself between Nelson, who was aggressive and trying to throw punches, and Mr. Ramirez. Hank told Nelson to leave and also told him that the sheriffs had been called.

As Brandon and Steve got closer to Kelley, he pulled out a knife, swung and stabbed Brandon on the right side of his neck. Seconds before that, Steve had glanced back towards the Tavern and when he turned back around saw a mass of people pushing, shoving and fighting. Steve was unaware at that moment that Brandon had been stabbed. Steve grabbed the first person he saw who was not a bouncer: Kelley. Kelley sliced Steve across the jaw, just inches from his neck and wounded him in the chest. Steve tackled him to the ground. At no time did Kelley tell Steve that he had a weapon or to stay away from him. Steve explained to us later that it felt like brass knuckles or something very hard hitting his jaw. "Everything happened very fast," he said.

Herb had headed towards the altercation involving Nelson, Mr. Ramirez, and Hank but saw that it is under control. He turned back and heard Brandon yell, "Blood, Blood!" Herb said Brandon was about 15 feet from him and sounded nervous but Herb did not see any blood at that point. Brandon called out that someone had a knife and then grabbed this throat with both hands. Herb said Brandon now had "a lot" of blood coming through his hands. Brandon fell to his knees and then to the pavement. Herb saw Steve on the ground struggling with Kelley and tried to get the knife out of Kelley's hand. Steve had also heard Brandon yell, "Blood, Blood!" He let go of Kelley, ran to Brandon and saw that he was bleeding profusely. Steve held his hand over the wound in Brandon's neck. With every heartbeat Brandon's wound gushed.

Steve got off of Kelley to go to Brandon so abruptly that Herb suddenly found himself flat on his back and Kelley was now standing over him. He felt like he was losing his grip on Kelley. As Herb fought to get the knife away, the knife closed on Herb's hand cutting him severely, severing a tendon that effects movement in the index finger. He kicked Kelley who fell backwards and dropped the knife. Herb grabbed the knife and Kelley took off running.

Even injured, Herb did a great job of preserving the knife. The knife was turned into a deputy and the deputy was advised that the knife had been used in the attack. This was significant because a lot of the time the authorities do not recover the weapon used in a crime. The knife was eight inches in length when opened. It had a four inch curved blade. Kelley's knife had the type of blade that folds into the handle and had to be opened manually.

While Herb still had the knife, he used it to pierce the tires of the white Saturn belonging to Nelson's girlfriend. Herb did not want anyone to get away in that car. He believed that the friends of Nelson and Kelley were in that white car.

Later during the vehicle inspection, the chief investigator saw puncture marks and asked that the inside of the tires be tested for blood to compare it to Herb, Brandon, Steve and Kelley. It was impressive that Herb had the foresight to think of puncturing the tires.

The positive thing to come of this, as far as the case is concerned, is that the DNA comparison to Brandon was a match to what was found inside the tire. This was one of two links between Brandon, the knife, and Kelley that was significant. It showed that the knife was the murder weapon and, even though it had been thrust into two tires, DNA was still left behind.

Later, Kelley initially denied anything to do with a knife, lie number one on his part. However, this was hard to refute after his DNA along with Brandon's, Steve's and Herb's was found on the knife by forensic science. He later testified that he "used the knife for work and for other stuff." Kelley was a journeyman roofer by trade. The District Attorney asked him during the trial if he had planned to do any roofing jobs on New Year's Eve, to which he answered, "No."

The bouncers realized that Brandon was hurt and turned all their attention to him so Kelley saw a chance to leave. Ms. Fowler, in bare feet at that point, presumably stepped in Brandon's blood as she and Kelley fled the scene.

Steve continued holding Brandon's neck to try and stop the bleeding but the knife had severed an artery and the blood was coming too fast. One of the bouncers, Bryan, a corpsman in the Navy, got a medical bag from his car and he too, tried to help his friend.

We found out later that the knife not only severed an artery but damaged his windpipe, as well. If the wound was held to stop the flow of blood, Brandon could not breathe. If the wound was not held tightly the blood poured out. Bryan's heart was breaking because he knew there was nothing he could do. Brandon's wound was grave. There was such agony in his voice and in his eyes as he told us of his efforts to help Brandon. At one point, Brandon took Bryan's hand and pushed it tightly up against his wound. Bryan stated that Brandon was able to communicate somewhat right up until the paramedics came. This might have been due to the fact that it was not the carotid artery that was severed but the artery that controlled the blood flow to the thyroid. For a time, blood was still flowing to his brain but with every heartbeat the volume of blood pumping decreased. As blood continued to pour out of the wound, Brandon began shaking and went into shock. Bryan testified that a white car (presumably the white Saturn) speed past the two of them, almost hitting them as he and Brandon were on the ground.

Paramedics arrived and Brandon was transported to Mission Community Hospital, which is a trauma center. He went into cardiac arrest in the ambulance. Since all reports were considered evidence it wasn't until after the trial that we were told that every effort was made to save our son.

At the hospital, Brandon was given four units of blood and CPR was performed. The doctors also attempted to give him an airway. He arrived at Mission Hospital with no respirations and after about 20 minutes was pronounced dead.

The severity of Brandon's stab wound was not compatible with life from the moment it happened. If the stabbing had occurred in front of a hospital with a vascular surgeon standing right there, complete with all his instrumentation, Brandon might have survived. Even then the blood loss was too great and too fast.

Steve and Herb were treated for their wounds and later released. Both will forever bear the scars of that night. Steve has a vivid scar on his jaw and on his chest and both boys, along with many others, watched their good friend as he lay dying.

The parking lot of the bar became a crime scene and it was only recently that I could even go there. It took me two years to feel I had the courage to face it. Even then, it was not a planned visit. Riley and I were in the area watching Sean play rugby and as we got close to the bar's location, Riley asked if I wanted to see it. I had never been to the bar; Brandon could not socialize with us when he was working and it was far enough from our home that we had no other reason to go.

It will always haunt me that I was not able to comfort my son that night. He must have been so very frightened and in pain and I was not there. I understand that while he could still speak he pleaded with Bryan not to let him die. I have been assured that if he felt pain it would not have been for long. Shock set in from all the blood loss, but that knowledge does little to comfort me. For all intents and purposes, our son died in a handicapped parking space in the parking lot of a bar, for no other reason than a stupid argument and the poor judgment of two men.

After fleeing the parking lot in the burgundy Corolla, Kelley and his girlfriend drove back to Laguna Beach where they were staying for the weekend with another couple from the group. There, at the house in Laguna Beach, was Ms. Fowler's aunt, a Ms. Wilson, who came with them for the weekend but did not join the group at the bar that night.

Four of the friends, one of which was Ms. Wilson's son, drove away from the bar in the white Saturn but only made it as far as a close by gas station before they had to stop due to the slashes in the tires. We understand that AAA was called and while Nelson's girlfriend Ms. Barrs waited for assistance, the three others walked back to the parking lot of the Tavern, I assumed, to see what they could find out about what was going on there. Nelson and Mr. Scott were still back at the parking lot, having been detained by sheriff's deputies for questioning. They were later released.

Once back at the house in Laguna Beach, Ms. Fowler stated that she received a call, (I believed from one of the other girls in their group), and was told that someone had been hurt at the Tavern. She and Kelley were encouraged to leave the house. Kelley wanted to go back to his house in Big Bear. Since he and Ms. Fowler had been drinking that night, Ms. Wilson offered to drive them back in the Corolla to her house in Hesperia. Kelley changed his clothes and the trio left Laguna Beach.

At some point, and it is unclear whether it was while they were still at the Laguna Beach house or on the way to Hesperia, Kelley was informed that someone had died. Even knowing that, Kelley and his girlfriend slept in the car on the way to Hesperia and upon arrival there, went back to sleep at Ms. Wilson's house. They went to sleep! I shook my head in disbelief when I heard of this! How could he possibly sleep after what he had done?

Interestingly, the stories Kelley, his girlfriend, and their friends told changed from interview to interview and even while testifying in court their stories changed.

Kelley's arrest was a cooperative process with assistance from a couple of agencies. The Orange County Sheriff's Department had the assistance of the Fontana Police Department and the San Bernardino County Sheriff's Department (SBSD).

We learned that initially Kelley's friend Mr. Scott was not helpful to the sheriff's department but, after a time, they were able to locate addresses for Kelley, his girlfriend and his girlfriend's aunt, Ms. Wilson.

The other agencies from Fontana and San Bernardino went immediately to those locations to keep an eye out. Fontana police spoke with Nelson's girlfriend's mother who told them Ms. Barrs was driving the white Saturn. It was confirmed that the burgundy Corolla belonged to Kelley and Ms. Fowler. In fact, they had only purchased the new car together a couple of week's prior.

Nelson's girlfriend, Ms. Barrs was not that cooperative with investigators either when they arrived in Fontana. Eventually she told them that Kelley and Ms. Fowler were on their way with Ms. Wilson to her home in Hesperia. San Bernardino sheriff's deputies went to that location but did not initially make contact at the request of the investigators from Orange County. The investigators merely wanted them to make sure the burgundy Corolla was still in the driveway, which it was.

San Bernardino deputies watched the house from a distance and waited for the arrival of Orange County authorities.

The investigators, including the chief investigator, were on their way to Hesperia and were also in the process of getting a search warrant. I believe they did not want anyone to spook the occupants into destroying evidence before they could get there. Plans changed when the San Bernardino Sheriff's Department advised investigators that Kelley and his girlfriend were loading the car and appeared to be getting ready to leave. The SBSD were asked to hold the occupants in the front yard and secure the home and await the investigators arrival.

Kelley was taken into custody very quickly and initially told the police that he "got in a fight in Orange County, and I messed up." He was ultimately charged with murder, attempted murder and assault with a deadly weapon.

I wanted to include information regarding the law enforcement organizations that came to the aid of Orange County investigators that day. The public does not always know what goes on behind the scenes. When something bad like this happens, all the agencies work together no matter where they are from. The San Bernardino Sheriff's Department dropped everything that day to take action and make sure no one left the Hesperia location. Our family is eternally grateful to all agencies involved in this case. It truly was a team effort.

Ms. Wilson was also arrested at her home that morning along with Kelley, for accessory after the fact. She cleaned off the (bloody) foot pedal in Kelley's car and knowingly destroyed evidence. Remember, I stated that Ms. Fowler was bare foot as she and Kelley left the bar. She had stepped in blood that was most likely Brandon's. Blood was left behind on the pedal after she drove the Corolla back to Laguna Beach as well as on the floor mat in the back seat while she and Kelley were passengers later. She stated in court that she never looked at her feet that morning and was unaware of anything on her feet, which seemed unlikely to me.

I understand that Ms. Wilson's reasoning for destroying evidence was that she didn't want any trouble. Kelley's girlfriend could not be linked to the actual murder and was not arrested, only questioned.

Kelley's girlfriend, Ms. Fowler told investigators that Ms. Wilson washed Kelley's clothes and burned a bloody tank top in the fireplace. During the search of the home we understand there was evidence of recently burnt material in the fireplace but investigators were unable to determine what it was before it burned.

Nelson was not arrested at the scene but was later indicted on the same charges, on the grounds that he was culpable and that he aided and abetted his friend Kelley. He was considered, in the eyes of the law, just as guilty. He instigated the whole incident by his actions inside and outside of the bar. At no time did he stop his aggressiveness, convince Kelley to stop, or give any indication that he felt it was time to leave.

The chief investigator told me that Nelson felt he had been "superiorly disrespected" that night. Was that his justification for his involvement in the confrontation at the sports bar? He was also very concerned about his "grill" as it is called, or "teeth jewelry." Grills are pricey and he wanted it back. Several witnesses positively identified Nelson as the one wearing the grill. It was found on the pavement at the bar parking lot and therefore held as evidence. His "grill" also linked him to the scene.

Nelson ended up in Central California prior to his arrest and I believe that some how he found out that he had been indicted and was encouraged to turn himself in to Orange County investigators at a Greyhound bus station, which he did, without incident.

Many have asked why Nelson was detained at the scene that night and released if it was felt he was suspect. As I noted before, at the beginning of an investigation there are mostly questions that need to be answered and the investigators were waiting for all the evidence. The Grand Jury indicted Nelson based on that evidence.

What Do We Do Now?

The next days were a blur. January 1st of 2007 was a Monday. Because Brandon's death was ruled a homicide, his body was automatically transported to the Orange County Coroner's Office directly from the hospital. An autopsy was performed that morning at 9:03 a.m. We did not find out until the trial exactly what was in that report. In later conversations with our chief investigator I learned that he, personally was present at the autopsy. We knew how Brandon died, but what else, if anything, would the coroners report reveal?

Waiting for updates was one of the hardest parts for our family. Not much information that was to be included in the trial was shared with us, most everything was considered evidence and therefore confidential.

The coroner, who had performed over 4,700 autopsies, stated that the horizontal wound described in his report as a stab, was in the middle of the neck towards the right side. He stated the weapon used was a single edged knife.

On internal exam of Brandon's neck he noted that the wound was one and a half to two inches in length and about and one and one quarter inches deep. There was damage to his windpipe and the knife completely transected, or sliced through, the thyroid artery, which is about the width of a pencil. Death, he stated in court, would be in minutes. We found out during the trial that all toxicology tests performed on our son were negative.

Another sad task we had that first day was to call our pastor. Brandon's funeral was planned for later in the week but the day would hinge on when his body would be released from the coroner, something that was out of our control. My friend Kathy set up an appointment with the mortuary and went with us so we would not make hasty or overly emotional decisions about the burial. The mortuary was so helpful and made the process more bearable and Kathy's gentle guidance was so appreciated.

The reality that our son was gone was just too much to fathom! Brandon was only 21! He had hopes and dreams! He had a whole life to live and there we sat in a mortuary, picking out a casket, ordering death certificates and looking at headstones. This just could not be happening! We were still thinking he would just walk through the door, say "Hey", throw himself on the couch and ask what there was to eat! The idea that he was never coming back was just not sinking in even as we made choices at the mortuary.

Brandon was tall. At 6'3", there was concern that he would not fit in a standard size casket. A longer one was ordered as a standby just in case. The casket size did not turn out to be a problem. We learned that if the casket had been a bit small they would have had to "fit him in". He would certainly not know the difference, and the reasonable part of us knew that, but the emotional part of us did not want him to have to be "fit" into the casket.

Part of our visit to the mortuary included picking out a headstone, or marker, as they called it. Then we had to decide what would be engraved on it. The final decisions regarding the marker were not made that day but soon after. We were too overwhelmed with all the other choices we had to make that day and knew we had time for our options regarding his marker. The biggest decision we faced was choosing what type of stone used. For Brandon we chose beautiful black granite with blue flecks. Other decisions included the size for the headstone, and any words, symbols or pictures that might be incorporated and the size and font for any lettering. Several examples were emailed to us before the final decision was made. The marker actually takes months to be delivered to the gravesite. Along with his full name and birth and death years, we chose to have a Celtic cross on the left side of the marker and also a color picture of Brandon on the right. The picture was covered with a clear protective gloss of some kind for protection from the elements, especially from the sun. Riley composed what would be engraved on it. The marker reads:

"He touched so many lives and we are all better for having known him. Sleep in peace warrior."
"Blessed are the peacemakers" Matthew 5:9

There was never a question in our minds that we would bury Brandon rather than cremate him. We wanted a place we could go to feel closer to him. We knew it is just his body there but it is what we wanted. We were fortunate that my sister-in law Dianna works for the Cemetery District in our county. Her office is located just inside the entrance of the memorial park where Brandon is buried.

The district owns and operates all three of our counties public cemeteries. To have someone we love, there to help us during a time when we were so frozen in our grief was such a blessing. We will never forget her attention to us during a time when she was grieving the loss of her nephew as well.

A viewing was planned at the mortuary for that Thursday evening and the funeral for the next morning, Friday January 5th. We prayed that the coroner would release Brandon's body in time. We were told that after the autopsy there was at least a 48 hour waiting period after which the body is re-examined to make sure nothing was missed, no new bruising or wounds found.

We knew a large group of people would want to attend the viewing and the staff was so accommodating and our representative at the mortuary so very compassionate and sympathetic. I cannot say enough about how delicately we were treated. Dianna was also instrumental in guiding us to him.

Looking back as I write this, our family was so fortunate in a lot of ways during a time when one cannot even think straight. We were treated so thoughtfully by so many when we were distraught, tired, scared and so very sad. There were countless acts of kindness shown to us after Brandon's murder.

Erin White

Those First Few Days

Brandon's friends were all in shock, his death affecting them all so intensely and so deeply. Josh and Patrick and many others decided to raise money to help us with funeral expenses so memorial t-shirts were prepared and sold. All the t-shirts designed had Brandon's picture on them. One of a kind t-shirts were made for Riley, Sean, Colleen and I. Mine had a picture of Brandon, Sean and me. It was the last photo taken of just the three of us. In the picture I am sitting between the boys on a couch, our arms entwined as we waited to be seated for Thanksgiving brunch.

Countless friends and family gathered for the fundraisers at Hennessey's in Dana Point, a favorite hang out of all the kids. Brandon had been a bouncer there as well.

The first event was Tuesday evening; the second night after Brandon was murdered. I don't know how Riley and I got the strength to go. Our friends and next-door neighbors, Jason and Michelle offered to drive us that day. We wanted to go in support of all who gathered there and to have those closest to Brandon around us.

In front of Hennessey's a table was set up with candles and pictures of Brandon. Posters and banners hung everywhere and were filled with signatures of all who attended. The love we felt was immeasurable. Brandon's friends made enough money through the t-shirt sales and donations to pay the funeral expenses, which were over $15,000.00. There was money left over and after discussing it, Riley and I decided to put the money in a special account and started a scholarship fund in Brandon's name at his alma mater, El Toro High School. The scholarship is called The Brandon White Scholarship Award. It is a scholarship that is given to a worthy high school Senior Varsity football player to aid him in starting out in college.

We have given out three scholarships so far and hope to continue the tradition as long as we can. Because of the love Brandon's friends had for him and for our family this scholarship has been made possible. All who have donated are helping a worthy high school Senior continue his education.

The coaches choose the scholarship recipient with Riley giving his input. The award goes to the player who loves the game the most. A dedicated and team inspiring player who may be first in the gym to work out and the last to leave. Generally the award goes to the player who shows the most heart.

The first of the two gatherings at Hennessey's was shown on the local news. I remember seeing it all on TV and being amazed to see the amount of people that attended. I think every one of his friends must have been as well as many of our friends and family.

Sean had driven Brandon's black Dodge Ram truck to the bar that night and it was parked in front of Hennessey's. On the hood, the boys had laid several Hennessey's security shirts and they had all signed them. Later in the evening one of Brandon's friends, Troy, stood up on Brandon's big truck and said this Viking prayer:

"Lo, there do I see my father,
Lo, there do I see my mother
and my sisters and my brothers.
Lo, there do I see the line of my people,
back to the beginning!
Lo, they do call to me.
They bid me take my place among them,
In the halls of Valhalla!
Where the brave may live, forever!"

Brandon was partly of Nordic decent, on his dad's side (and thanks to me partly Irish as well) and very proud of his heritage. One of his favorite movies of all time was "The 13th Warrior" with actor Antonio Banderas. He must have watched it a million times. This Viking prayer was recited during the movie. I don't know for sure but I think that is where he may have heard the prayer the first time. It was very powerful to hear it that night. I still remember it vividly and it meant so much.

There are a many things that stick out in my mind about those two evenings at Hennessey's. One involves a woman named Karen, whom I had never met before. She walked up to me that first night and told me that she did not know me or know Brandon but had been compelled to come because her son had been killed similarly to Brandon. She handed me a picture of her son, and her phone number and told me to call her when I was up to it.

I remember thinking how wonderful it was that this nice lady was reaching out to me. How moving it was that she took the time to go to a gathering where she would know no one just to meet me. Although, at the time I felt I had all I could do to cope, I remember thinking "I don't have room for anyone else in my life right now." I was however, so touched at her gesture, our shared grief and her kind spirit.

What I didn't know was that this was a woman that understood exactly what I was feeling. She was exactly who I NEEDED to talk to, but of course I couldn't see that then. Her son had been murdered a year before Brandon had and in a very violent way, as he made a call on his cell phone outside a bar in San Clemente, California. You could see the sadness in her face as she spoke to me about her son.

I did call her days later but got her voice message and didn't leave my phone number. I wanted to be in control of when we had our conversation rather than leaving my number and not knowing when she might be able to call back. I was relieved, really that she didn't answer that first time, and I later told her that. I was just not ready to talk to her but felt I should at least be kind and attempt to call. It would be many months before I called back. I am sorry now I waited so long. All the while, she waited patiently for me to come to her.

In Karen, I found a friend and someone who really understood everything I was feeling. I told her of my hesitancy in calling her. She said she had felt the same way, beside herself and overwhelmed, just like I did. She told me more about her son Jason and I told her of Brandon.

I hope that I can someday lend support to another the way she lent support to me. Maybe that is partly why I write this now. To offer what I know about the worst tragedy a parent can endure. To let others know that they are not alone in their feelings.

Another event from the fundraisers that stands out in my mind is regarding a man that I never got to meet. He was inside Hennessey's while we were outside and a regular patron of the bar. I was told by the other bouncers that Brandon used to get mad at him for drawing on the big white cloth napkins they had. I was lucky enough to be given a napkin that he had drawn on.

On it was a portrait of Brandon, done with a plain black ink pen. It was an amazing likeness of Brandon, a beautiful drawing of his head and shoulders. It took up the whole eighteen-inch square white napkin. Brandon has a slight smile on his face and a halo above his head and angel wings. One arm is up with the index finger pointing up, as if to say, "Quit drawing on the napkins!" At the bottom it reads "My condolences to you and your family. Your son was a good guy and a respectful man." He signed and dated it as well. I am sorry I have never met the man who drew it. I have since framed it between two pieces of glass and it hangs in our bedroom. I will always treasure it and smile everyday when I look at it.

As the week wore on, food appeared on our doorstep. Hot soup, rolls, salad, chicken and more, with no name just left at the door with love. We were so very thankful because food was not something we had even thought about and there were constantly people in the house. My employers quickly sent a gift certificate for a company called "Restaurants on the Run". We ordered food from local restaurants and it was delivered. We so appreciated being able to just call and order food especially when all during the week we never knew who might stop by.

My friend Jennifer, a physician in the area did something for us I will never forget. She, with newborn in her arms, delivered a cooler full of food she had cooked. Enchiladas, salad, soup, brownies, macaroni and cheese, you name it. She told me that she wanted to do something and flowers did not seem enough, so she "cooked". I was so touched that she took the time to do that for us especially since the baby in her arms was her third child!

Riley and I had the difficult task of going to the condo Brandon shared with Josh to decide what clothes Brandon would be buried in. Many of their friends were there, staying with Josh. As we sadly went through his things, we searched and searched for a ring that Brandon cherished. We wanted Brandon to be buried in the ring he so loved. It was a ring that he wore all the time and given to him by his dad. The silver ring with a thunderbird engraved on it had actually been Riley's. Bran's girlfriend, Regan thought he never wore it to work though. The ring was nowhere to be found. I was upset that we could not bury him with it. Where could it be, we wondered? We did settle on a favorite pair of jeans, a long sleeved shirt he wore a lot and another silver ring he had. I am sad however, that none of us remembered to include his beloved rainbow sandals.

For three days our local news channels covered the story of Brandon's murder. His death was the tragic story on the nightly news only to be replaced by another family's tragedy a few days later. I tried to tape as many of the broadcasts as I could and have watched them over and over.

Our doorbell rang one afternoon two days after the murder and there stood a reporter from Channel 11 News wanting to know if she could interview us about what had happened to Brandon. We agreed to the interview but I requested that they accept a picture of Brandon that was clearer than the ones being shown on TV. I am not sure where the media got the pictures that were being shown but they were not very clear.

Lighting was brought in to our living room and microphones were clipped on. The microphone wire was run under our shirt and attached at our shirt collar. As it happened, Sean was not home at the time, so it was just Riley, Colleen and I. We sat on the couch as the reporter asked us about Brandon. I wondered why the she was dressed so casually if she was to go on TV. I found out later she just does the interviewing.

The cameraman who filmed the whole interview then put his camera (with a huge lens) very close to a current portrait of our three kids that I took right off the wall for him. The picture was a Christmas gift from all three and taken just a month before. I appreciated the fact that a less grainy picture would be shown on the news.

During the interview I said, "I couldn't believe some one could do something like that to Brandon." Riley said that given a chance to do it all over, Brandon still would have gone in to help. Colleen did not speak but softly whispered and nodded in agreement to what I had said. The interview was later edited and the nightly news anchors read it. The interviewer was nowhere to be seen in the edited portion. We do not even remember hearing her voice asking us the questions, just our answers. It was an interesting process to experience. We were not prepared for the knock on the door so my first thought was "I must look horrible." Imagine thinking that with all we were going through! We heard the interview was on several different stations that night.

Prior to the New Year, Brandon and Herb had been re-laying all the intra locking bricks we had in our back yard. In the months since Riley originally had placed them it had rained a few times and they settled unevenly, which was not uncommon. The boys said they would take them all up and re-lay them for some extra money. All of our patio furniture was piled by our front door so they could work. You could barely get to our front door.

The work would never get finished by them. They had gotten all the bricks back down but had not swept all the fine sand between the bricks to hold them in place or done the final cleanup and replacement of the furniture to the back yard.

Unbeknownst to us and while Riley and I were at Brandon's condo picking out the clothing he was to be buried in, our friends Guy and Joe were at our house sweeping all the sand between the bricks and repositioning the furniture in the backyard. We didn't know how we were going to get it all done with all that was going on and worried about all the people who would be coming back to the house after the funeral. How could we possibly handle having people come to the house with the backyard the way it was and furniture by the front door? These two great people saved us with their act of compassion and we will never forget it.

It was not until the very day of the viewing, four days after Brandon was murdered, that the coroner released his body to the mortuary.

We came to find out that the mortuary was instrumental in the release of Brandon's body. They kept calling and calling and finally were able to go and get his body released, only about three hours before the viewing. It was a very tense time for us. In the back of our minds, we knew there was a chance that the coroner would not release his body that day. There were preparations of Brandon's body that the mortuary had to have time to do and we are so thankful to them for working so fast to accommodate us. We were told that Brandon's body was embalmed before reaching the mortuary so that time consuming process did not have to be done. However, the choice to embalm his body or not was yet another decision out of our control. I found out later that if there is to be a formal viewing, embalming is a requirement.

The viewing was the first time we saw Brandon. The public viewing was set for 7 p.m. The family's private viewing was set for 4 p.m. so that we could make sure that we were ok with the way he looked. Regan asked if she could go with us to the private viewing and I said ok as long as the four of us went in first. Of course, she agreed without question.

We entered the room that afternoon and there were floral arrangements everywhere. One of the boys, Brian a long time friend, had made a beautiful wooden cross with a wreath surrounded by flowers and a picture of Brandon in the middle. It stood on a pedestal and was lovely. We still have it.

As we approached the casket, I was very nervous. Bran looked as if he were asleep. I remember thinking that he looked so small to me. The wound on his neck had been cosmetically covered up but we could still tell where it was. Remember, we were not able to see him until the viewing and only knew what the investigators and the bouncers told us regarding his wounds.

His hands were crossed across his abdomen and I asked why they looked blotchy. I was told that when he fell back to the ground they had become scraped and makeup was used to conceal it.

I stroked his hair and I remember thinking that his face was so cold. I felt his chest and it was also very cold and hard. You are so used to seeing your son in life with his chest full with air and there he was, lifeless in a casket.

Brandon's body had been kept refrigerated so of course it would be cold, I thought. He looked peaceful though. My lips had a waxy taste on them long after we left the mortuary that night from kissing his forehead so much. I could not resist kissing him. I assumed the taste that remained on my lips was from the make up the mortuary uses. Regan came in and joined us after a time. Her face was so full of sadness, her eyes full of tears. We all just stood there looking at Brandon. I had requested that he not be shaven if at all possible. He had a slight goatee and just slight stubble but it was how he looked the day he died and I did not want them to shave him, and they didn't.

We had asked the mortuary if the bouncers and his close friends could come in prior to the public viewing to have some time with Brandon. Of course it was fine. There was no request we made that was not allowed. They were so obliging, so understanding, so caring.

Recommending a mortuary is not something that is typically a topic of conversation but O'Connor Mortuary was so compassionate and kind. They had a job to do this is true, but, the whole sad, emotional event was handled with such gentleness and I personally will never forget it.

There was quite a crowd for the viewing. The mortuary staff said it was one of the largest they had ever had. Many of our loved ones were there. Brandon's childhood friend Brian with whom he shared a very strong bond was there. Brandon and Brian had been fast friends since kindergarten and his mom Pam, my friend for as long. They flew in from Colorado and it meant so much to have them with us.

Beloved Dr. May, who delivered both Brandon and Colleen, was there. With him were many of the doctors I work with and many, many coworkers. I will never forget the sadness in Dr. May's eyes at seeing the boy he brought into this world now in a casket.

Both of our families, our friends and Brandon's friends were there to lend their support. Brandon's football coaches from both high school and college were there and brought helmets for the top of the casket. Their eyes were swimming in tears and their hearts heavy.

I did not want to leave. I knew it would be the last time I would ever see Brandon. We greeted everyone who came, hugged many, many people but we were dying inside. It was so unreal. My mind could just not accept that the boy lying there was our son, our baby, our Brandon!

After everyone had left, the mortuary staff allowed us to stay as long as we wanted to. It meant so much to have that time. The mortuary asked if we wanted all the items placed so lovingly in the casket to be forever sealed inside and we said, yes!

Many mementos were placed in the casket with Brandon as friends and family filed through. I put in the picture of Brandon and myself taken in San Clemente on the pier.

Riley, Sean and Colleen also placed something personal in the casket. Along with our items there were many that his friends and our families added as well; a cell phone was placed by his hand and I still don't know whose it was. I think it might have been Steve's but I have never asked him. I felt whomever had placed it there it must have had a private reason for doing so.

There were cigars and some of Brandon's favorite CD's and also his ever-present chap stick. One of his security shirts that had been signed by many of the guys was placed inside as well. Guy had arranged for us to have an Orange County Sheriff's badge, the type that is sewn onto the arm of a uniform. Brandon had hoped to earn one some day. That was placed in the casket along with many pictures and lots and lots of personal notes and of course, a bottle of New Castle beer.

We finally headed home still feeling like we were in a bad dream that we all just wanted to wake up from. The kind of bad dream that you are so happy to awaken from to find it was just a dream. Only we were not waking up.

The Funeral

The day of the funeral, January 5th 2007, dawned cold and windy. The pallbearers, Sean, Steve and Herb as well as friends, Patrick (Pat), Jerod and Blake were quiet and thoughtful as we waited in the pastor's office before the service.

In honor of "Whitey", (the nickname Brandon was given in high school), many of us wore white ribbons pinned to our clothes that day.

All the pallbearers also wore a dog tag type necklace with a laser image of Brandon on it. Blake arranged for Colleen and I to have one and I still wear mine everyday. It is another way I keep Brandon with me and I get many comments on it.

My good friend Deb and her son, Nico, lovingly put together a DVD slide show to music that played inside the church as loved ones arrived. I had given Deb albums and pictures still in frames for her to use as she wished. Steve and the boys put together their own disk and without having much time the two disks were combined by Nico just before the service.

The slide presentation was amazing. I have copies of both disks but cannot seem to bring myself to watch them again. I want to but can't seem to make that step. Maybe because within all those pictures are too many memories and I find it too painful to know that there will be no more memories created with Brandon.

The slide show played as everyone gathered in the church so I really didn't get to see all of it at the time. As I wrote this paragraph, I stopped for a minute and gazed outside wondering again what is keeping me from watching them. I really do want to see all the pictures again. I guess it is hard to knowingly watch something that will most certainly make me sad no matter how badly I long to see them.

The church was filled beyond capacity. We had warned Pastor Greg that there might be a large crowd. He had thought ahead and borrowed chairs from neighboring churches but even with the extras there were still not enough places to sit. People were everywhere; those who did not have a chair stood or sat on the floor.

Together at the church in Brandon's honor, family and friends, former coaches and team mates, teachers and principals, co-workers and schoolmates. We were told that more than 600 people attended that day. Our pastor allowed everyone to sit wherever they could. Many sat up by the altar but there were those who had to listen from outside.

As Riley, Sean, Colleen and I waited in the pastor's office, a "friend of a friend" of Brandon's arrived unexpectedly, dressed in his kilt and carrying his bagpipes. He had cleared his schedule and offered to play if we wanted him to. Brandon LOVED the bagpipes and we were so thrilled to have him! The casket was carried into the church to "Scotland the Brave", beautifully played on an instrument Brandon admired so much. At our request, "Going Home", was also played as the boys carried the casket out of the church. I have never seen the bagpiper since that day but will never forget his kindness.

Pastor Greg spoke so eloquently. He spoke of how, in Brandon's truck, we found his bible, marked at Matthew 5:9 "Blessed are the Peacemakers." That scripture was sort of adopted by all of us after that. Brandon wanted to be a peacemaker and I know he was inspired by those words. When working at the bar, I am told, he tried to defuse altercations with patrons using words, rather than force.

Sean and Colleen got up in front of all those people and spoke from their hearts and I am so proud of them for doing it. When Sean walked up to the podium, he was carrying a boom box, and before he spoke he turned it on and played a song I had never heard before that day. I remember thinking it odd that he would choose to play a song and kept trying to catch his attention to say "ok Sean turn it off, that's enough." He, of course didn't, and the entire song played. The group My Chemical Romance titled it, "Welcome to the Black Parade."

Later I asked Sean why he chose that song and he said simply that it was a song he had asked Brandon to listen to and they had both liked it. The song is about a man dying of cancer at a young age. His happiest memory was of his father taking him to a parade as a young boy. Death comes to the man in the form of his best memory, the black parade, and a metaphor for death. The words of the song struck me differently. I heard the words "savior of the beaten and the damned" and "we'll carry on" and thought of Brandon. I also heard, "I'm just a man I'm not a hero", and that touched me too. Songs can often be interpreted in many ways, which is the beauty of music.

After the song finished there were tears a plenty in the church. I remember looking around and seeing so many of his friends crying and thinking that even though, at the time, I did not understand what the song was about, it obviously affected them all very deeply. I have since downloaded that song and have listened to it over and over.

My niece Keighley, at Riley's request, played "Amazing Grace" on the piano that day. She was very nervous but played beautifully and with such heart. Everyone in the room was so moved and we were so thankful she had agreed to play.

I did not try and address the group that day, I couldn't. It would have taken a strength that I just did not possess. I was sure I would not be able to hold myself together. We had agreed ahead of time on the speakers besides Sean and Colleen. There were so many that wanted to say something but it was decided that we had to have a limit or the service would have lasted all day. Regan asked if she could say a few words. Brandon's friend Blake came up to the podium by himself and shared some funny stories about Brandon. Patrick, Herb and Jerod all stood together and spoke about their friend.

Pastor Greg just let everyone talk. I will be forever grateful to our pastor for just letting us all remember Brandon in our way and for opening his church to so many.

I recall being so worried about my little mom that day. We were seated on the end of the first aisle and the doors to the church were open so as many as possible could be inside. The wind was blowing furiously up the middle of the church and I had my arms around my mom to keep her warmer. I was so happy she was there with me. She has a hard time getting around and it meant a lot to have her by my side.

I looked around and saw so much love and so much sorrow at the same time. From where I sat I tried to look around at everyone in attendance but it was very difficult. I am sorry still that I did not get to see and speak to every person there that day.

As the bagpiper led the casket out, we all followed. I was trying so hard to keep my composure. As we waited for the casket to be placed in the coach, I turned around and there was our dentist, Dr. Crosby and his sister Diane whom we have known for many years. Never in my life will I forget the stricken looks I saw. Their sadness for our family was written on their faces. Dr. Crosby had been Brandon's dentist all his life and it meant so much that the two of them were present that day.

My good friends, Tracy and Kelly, Michelle, Crystal and her husband Joe as well as my long time friend Ronald were faces I also remember seeing.

Old neighbors, current neighbors and my daughter's whole volleyball team, along with her coach, all dressed in uniform were there. All but three of the then twelve physicians I work with (some with their husbands or wives) attended. One doctor had to stay behind to cover the office and two were away on vacation. Many coworkers came in support. Some, as I am still learning, were there and I never knew.

Brandon's former principal from elementary school was there, along with two of Brandon's favorite teachers. Beloved Mrs. Martin, his 5th grade teacher (who also was Sean's teacher for two years) attended the service. Mrs. Martin called our house after she'd heard the tragic news of his death and asked Riley, "Was it our Brandon?" Mr. Johns, his 6th grade teacher, attended as well. Mr. Johns always addressed his students as "Mr. and Miss". He can also be credited with breaking all (or at least most) of his students from saying "um" between every other word, when speaking in class! No small feat! Brandon thought so highly of them both.

We never dreamed there would be so many people. We assumed that everyone would come back to our house. Some were only able to come for the actual funeral and had to get back home or to work. I wanted to take it all in, remember each and every person but some how I just couldn't. I felt bad when I was told later about somebody who was at the funeral and I'd had no idea. I wish I could show gratitude to every person who was there that day. Thank you to anyone who attended, in body or spirit.

We had arranged for a limo to transport the four of us to and from the church and cemetery. A private escort to the cemetery was arranged for the coach that carried the casket. As we waited at the church to be driven to the gravesite, my long time friend Gheida (who is also my hair stylist) and her husband Dominic (a Sergeant with the Orange County Sheriff's department), popped their heads inside the limo and just wanted to give us a hug. They are another couple I would have never known was there if they hadn't put themselves right in front of me and I was so glad they did.

We were very happy we had decided to have the escort because there was a line of cars that stretched at least two miles on the way to the cemetery. Having the escort kept the procession more organized. Hundreds of people then gathered close at Brandon's gravesite and the pastor spoke again. I had my hand on the edge of the casket the whole time and the sorrow I felt was overpowering. I really could not believe I was standing there in a cemetery with my hand on my son's casket. "This can not be real", I kept thinking to myself, even then.

Before Pastor Greg finished speaking, a great gust of wind swept through the cemetery. I know it sounds weird but it was like Brandon was letting us know he was there. Everyone gathered there looked at each other at that moment thinking the same thing I think. As quickly as the wind blew, it was gone. It was kind of eerie.

The four of us placed a rose on the casket. I kissed my hand then put my hand on the casket one more time. We had chosen a lovely spot to bury Brandon. Close to a tree that when it is full of leaves is so pretty.

Before we left Brandon's gravesite, a young man who had gone to high school with our son approached me. I believe he may have been a year or so behind Brandon. He was there to show his respect and handed me a pencil drawn picture he had done. It was Brandon's senior yearbook picture that he had drawn to an 8x10 portrait.

He told me that Brandon had always been nice to him and he wanted me to have the artwork. I was so touched and have never known who he was. The drawing was a wonderful likeness of Brandon and having it meant a lot to me.

As we left the cemetery many of Brandon's friends including Steve stayed to see the casket lowered into the ground. I have always thought it was their way of showing respect, staying and making sure everything was ok.

Friend Kathy came to the rescue once again and organized all the food back at our house. Kathy did not go to the gravesite so that she could get to our house ahead of everyone. Our mutual friend Kelly lent a hand as well. I honestly do not have a clue how they did it all. I knew the plan was for everyone to come back to our house but I can honestly say that I do not remember having anything to do with arranging any of it.

When I asked Kathy if it was ok to mention her name in what I was writing, her exact words were, "sure, but what did I do?" This is an example of how very blessed I am with her friendship. She really had no idea that we thought she had done such a great thing!

At our house food was in abundance. At the time, Sean was working for the restaurant chain Chili's. Brandon had also worked at the same location for a time but did not enjoy the restaurant business.

Sean's restaurant and another local Chili's brought appetizers by our house every hour, all arranged by his general manager.

It was amazing! Food just appeared! I had never considered what would happen when everyone came back at our house. Kathy and Kelly took care of everything and the appetizers just kept coming until we finally said "No More!"

Our house is not what you could consider big. About 1300 square feet but we packed about 250 people in that day. Our family will never forget Chili's kindness.

Our friend Earl told me later that there were so many people that as he stretched his arm out towards our dining room table to get some food it got caught in all the people. I had to smile at the vision of Earl's arm suspended straight out as he tried to get food!

Friend Troy brought a Viking horn, which was continuously filled with Mead (an ancient Viking drink) and passed around and around and around! I don't know how many times Riley and I took a turn, but I believe it was several! The horn was very big and as you lifted it to your mouth all you saw was a river of Mead coming at you!

Through it all Kathy and Kelly worked tirelessly. When Kathy's mom arrived and asked her if she was ok, that was when the enormity of the day hit Kathy and she broke down and cried. She had been so strong for me, had worked so hard, but the emotion of it all finally overtook her.

She had, after all, seen Brandon grow up. When the kids were little Kathy sat with me at the baby pool and never complained. She didn't have her own children then, (she now has three) but still sat with me. Every year that went by, my kids became better swimmers and we moved a bit closer to the "big" pool!

Amazingly, with wall-to-wall people inside and outside our house, only a single shot glass broke and just one picture on the wall had to be straightened. That was it! I do not remember even having to clean up! I am a clean up freak and I do not remember having to do anything!

It is interesting how the mind works. Some parts of that week are so vivid in my memory, but how everything came together at the house is still a blur. What I do know is how very lucky our family was to be enveloped by the loving arms of everyone that day.

Erin White

The Reality of Our Loss Sets In

There are a myriad of emotions that swirl around a family in grief. The pain of loss affected all of us in very different ways and at different times. As I have been writing of our experiences, this part has been the hardest part to start. Initially, there is just such sorrow and shock. Along with that was the disbelief that something like murder could be a part of our family's vocabulary.

I relied heavily on my friends. There was tons of loving support from all of them. I had lots of "ears" when I went back to work as well. My friends Karen, Mariann, Terri, Liz, Jenn and many others were always willing to hold me up. As the months wore, on I wondered if my friends were sick of me always wanting to talk about Brandon. I needed to talk about him and still do. I know for a fact that talking about him keeps him close and brings me comfort.

My friend and long time neighbor Deb, who always just seems to "get me" was, and still is such a great pal and calming influence. She and I have shared a multitude of emails, conversations and many glasses of wine. She and her family have lived across the street for many years. It was to her house that Colleen wanted to go that morning on January 1st. Deb lost her niece Stephanie just months after Brandon was murdered. Stephanie was involved in a fatal car accident in which the other party was drinking and driving. We understood the shock and sadness of a tragic and unnecessary loss of life.

My friends Sally and Crystal, whom I have known since the tender age of 18, have literally seen me grow up, marry and start a family. Both were and continue to be a much-needed support and I rely on their friendship and advice constantly.

My friend Michelle, in her own battle with cancer at the time, still made time for me. We shared many an email and while we were experiencing very different, scary and emotional times in our lives. These personal crises brought us even closer together.

Our close friends Joanne and Earl arrived at our house the day Brandon died with something to help me sleep and a shoulder to cry on. Joanne is also our family's doctor and a great cook as well. Brandon loved Joanne's Pansit. Pansit is a Filipino noodle dish that she

46

made when she knew Bran was coming over. She always sent him home with a big bag of it. He got the biggest grin on his face as she handed him his care package! She continued to make it in his honor at their annual Christmas party, just because she is a wonderful person and loved Brandon.

There was not a moment of the day where my thoughts did not stray to Brandon. I had trouble getting to sleep and once asleep, staying asleep. I woke every night for weeks at 2:30 a.m. (the time we got the phone call that night). I did try the sleeping aid Joanne had given me and it did help get me to sleep but I was still unable to rest the entire night. Riley also awoke during the night at the same time. Our hearts were broken. Brandon's death left a hole in our hearts and in our family. Our family dynamic was forever changed. Our lives forever changed because of the unthinkable acts of two men.

Our first thoughts were for our children, making sure they were ok. I rightly or wrongly suppressed my feelings of utter misery. In my mind, I felt I needed to be strong for them, strong for everyone.

Riley was very angry. He was angry and so sad at the same time. He was able to let out his emotion better than I could. He was so angry with Nelson for instigating the whole incident. Don't get me wrong, he understood who actually murdered our son but he felt that if the fight had never started and escalated due to Nelson's actions, Brandon would still be alive.

I remember the day of the funeral back here at the house. Colleen called to me and said that she was worried about her dad. She told me he was back in our bedroom. As I walked into the dressing area, Riley was on his knees in front of the sink, weeping as if his heart was breaking. He kept crying. "My baby boy, my baby boy." I just held him. I never seemed to find that sort of relief and I actually remembered at the time envying him for his ability to let go and allowing his emotions to over take him.

Sean took comfort in his friends and in Brandon's friends who surrounded him with care and love. That old cliché about alcohol making the pain go away was true for him at least part of the time. I worried about him a lot. I told him how I felt and he said not to worry he would not cause our family any more pain by doing anything stupid. His words did not convince me so I continued to worry and still do every day. Sean also had survivor's guilt. It is a very common occurrence in a case like this where the surviving sibling suffers horrible guilt, wondering why they lived and the other died. One afternoon on his way out of the house he told me there was not a day that went by that he did not wish it were he that had died. I remember very clearly the day he said that to me. I ached for him and told him I loved him and that I was glad he was here and never to talk like that again. Tears rolled down my cheeks as he walked away. How does a parent respond to words such as those? He felt that his brother had goals while he was still trying to figure out what to do with his life. Sean had not only lost his brother that night but also his best friend.

Theirs was a very close bond. He and Bran even got matching tribal tattoos on their arms. For as long as I could remember, the boys locked themselves in their room on Christmas Eve with my box of wrapping paper. For hours Riley and I heard them laughing and laughing. What was going on in there? On Christmas morning our gifts were "disguised" in boxes along with their socks and shirts, magazines and videos! Sean lost a part of himself the day Brandon died.

Colleen was much quieter in her grief. She was in the last half of her senior year of high school at the time. It was a tough semester for her and she had lots of trouble staying focused on school. She went to the gravesite almost daily during that semester. She missed her brother very much. Brandon always said he found her so annoying but he was her hero and she knew he would be there for her in an instant, and was.

Colleen was also much harder to read than Sean. She was so sad that Brandon would never see her graduate. It meant a lot to her that he attended the ceremony. She knew that it was not possible and it was very hard for her. She made a scrapbook of sorts with newspaper articles and pictures of her brother and his friends, along with many of the cards and other mementoes. She also designed two "You Tube" videos in honor of her brother. I have watched them over and over and from the number counts below the videos, so do many others. She did an amazing job! Her videos give me much comfort and I believe making all the remembrances of her brother helped her in her own grief.

I Am Not That Strong, Really!

I, myself, immediately took on the responsibility of mom, comforting everyone, making sure those around me were ok and as I look back, not allowing myself to grieve. I felt all of Brandon's friends were looking to me to be a mother figure. I know they never asked that of me but it was what I felt my role was. Maybe it was my way of keeping myself busy and not coming to terms with Brandon's death. Maybe it was because I really didn't want to believe he was gone. I was often asked, "How can you be so strong?" or "I would not be able to get out of bed, how do you do it?" One friend told me that he would be in his closet on the floor in the fetal position if it were he experiencing a loss such as ours. I thought to myself how wrong everyone was. I felt anything but strong. I cried often but mostly when I was alone. Now I wish I would have allowed myself to "lay in my closet on the floor in the fetal position."

I felt that if I let my guard down even a little, let myself feel the pain that was in my heart; I would just lose it and would not be able to get out of bed. My quest was to stay in control. If I stayed in control of my emotions I would not have a breakdown. Besides, I had two children who needed me, and a husband who needed me. I had all of Brandon's friends who needed me to be strong, or so I thought.

Looking back I feel it was my way to protect myself. So, I suppressed my feelings more and more. No one asked me to, no one expected it. I really wasn't trying to win a prize for being brave. If I had let go, as I should have, I was afraid I would start to cry and never stop. My emotions were like a big balloon. The tears were held in tight but sometimes leaked out. The rational part of me knows that it might have been ok to just let go but my mind would not let me.

I finally did have one breakdown of sorts. Colleen had talked about wanting to live with Riley's mom in San Diego for a while. I think it was her attempt to get away from all the sadness. She was trying to come to terms with among other things, the fact that her older brother was murdered and that he was never coming back. She was only 16 and her brother was killed in a violent way. We also still had the trial to endure. It struck me in such a heart wrenching way that she wanted to leave. I started sobbing uncontrollably. Riley just held me as I cried and cried and sorrowfully said that I was tired of being strong, tired of taking care of everyone. Losing control like that was a release of a sort but my utter misery still remained. Since no one had asked me to be strong I think I misled everyone who saw me. Outwardly, I seemed together and carried myself very well but I was actually dying inside.

Brandon's death also affected my ability to concentrate. After going back to work about two weeks after he died, I could not keep my thoughts from him. After all that we had been through and still faced, it was all I could do to get through the day. The level of fatigue was enormous and overpowering.

My friend and work partner Terri supported me in many ways more than she will ever know. I am sure I was little help at work for a very long time. She was a soft shoulder and a very good listener. She still is! She has also been so encouraging regarding my writing and has helped me edit and re-work paragraphs. Never once rolling her eyes when I admitted that I had spent another weekend working on "my book!"

My difficulty with concentration also affected something that I love, reading. I enjoy historical romance novels and fashion magazines the most. I found that I could not focus on any of it. I tried to read and my mind wondered to Brandon or to nothing at all. It is still difficult for me to enjoy reading and takes me months to get through a book instead of weeks and the magazines pile up unread until I give them away. I keep hoping someday I will be able to take pleasure in reading again.

I found that I became more of a homebody as well. Home was safe. I didn't have to be strong there. I didn't have to talk if I didn't want to. I have always been a social person so these "homebody" feelings were foreign to me. To prefer to be home was just not like me.

Brandon's death even affected my ability to inter-act with people. I think it is because I was uncomfortable about bringing up Brandon too much and making it painful for others because they often do not know what to say, or cannot relate to the fact that his death is something that our family will never "get over." I just recognized that there are those that I can feel relaxed about bringing him up at anytime and those who it is easier not to. I have to wonder if good intentioned people avoid the subject because they do not want to make us sad, but in reality this avoidance may save them from confronting their own fears at the thought of a loss such as ours. What our family has experienced is so intensely personal and all encompassing, the need to talk about it when we need to is quite vital. This is a topic I still struggle with. While I do not want to appear morose, the deep seeded ache in our hearts is often overwhelming.

And in Brandon's Corner...

We were contacted by the District Attorney's office very quickly, within a day or two of his murder and met a most wondrous man, Senior Deputy District Attorney Ebrahim (Brahim) Baytieh. He would be representing Brandon in court. Brahim was so caring and shared in our grief even before talking about anything to do with the trial.

He outlined what would happen. He said the road to justice was a long process but a fair one and it could be two years or more before it might go to trial. Riley and I looked at each other in disbelief that it might take two years. How wrong we were in the end! Brahim said he would do his very best to see justice served. He also said he would work very hard for us. We immediately liked and trusted him. He never disappointed us and our trust in him never once wavered.

I brought a picture of Brandon in a frame and gave it to Brahim that day. I wanted him to know what Brandon looked like in life. He said he would keep the photo in his office to remember whom he worked for. We had heard of Brahim and had read articles in the paper about murder cases in which he had been the prosecuting attorney. We felt so fortunate that he was on our side, but also were saddened that we would ever have a reason to meet him for this purpose.

The Chief Investigator, Joe Gaul, also contacted us almost immediately. He, too, got a middle of the night phone call that night and had to go to the murder scene. Joe had many hours of work ahead of him that day. He was a man that we also immediately liked and were so thankful for. He and his staff worked tirelessly and relentlessly to uncover the truth. He interviewed all the defendants and many others several times over. He made himself available to us with any questions and shared any information that he could. He received plenty of phone calls from us and was always willing to let us know how the investigation was progressing. We are grateful to call him friend.

I had mentioned earlier a ring that we were so disappointed we could not find among Brandon's things. All of his friends denied knowing its whereabouts. I decided to ask Joe if it could possibly be with all the evidence. Had Brandon really worn it to work even though he usually didn't? Joe got back to us a few days later and told us that the ring was indeed with the other pieces of evidence and that he would ask permission from the judge for it to be released. The judge gave his permission, the ring was photographed and Joe told Riley he could come and pick it up.

I was so excited to get the ring back. Riley came home with a manila envelope. I quickly opened it up and there was the ring. What I didn't know was that it still had blood on it. "Why wouldn't it?" I asked myself as I held the ring. Having never had to even think of things such as this, I was surprised and taken aback to see the blood, my son's blood on that ring. The ring he loved so much was on his finger when he died.

Your first thought would be to wash it, right? I couldn't and to this day, haven't. I cannot bring myself to. Riley would like the ring back since it was originally his but knows how I feel and will wait until I am ready. I would have thought it weird if a friend had told me that they had a ring with their son's blood on it in an envelope tucked away in a safe place. I feel it was a part of him, the last part of him that I have.

After a crime such as this the Victims Assistance department of the District Attorneys office also contacts the family. The Victims assistant keeps you posted regarding hearings and attends the hearings and the trial with you. They also offer support and information for the victim's family and friends. Our victim's assistant was Melissa all through the trial portion. Also, part of Melissa's function was to contact anyone we had agreed to give information to regarding the trial so that we did not have to make so many phone calls. Melissa was so helpful and such a comfort. She had quite a job organizing a group as large as ours.

Through the Victim's Assistance office, counseling is also available to the victim's family. The state pay's for this if you do not have insurance that will cover it or and in our case, reimbursed us for any co-payments. I understand prisoners who must pay restitution finance this. If a defendant is convicted of a crime, part of what he can earn in prison by working or money provided by the family for purchases from the prison canteen goes towards funding of this program. Colleen, Sean, and I went to counseling for a while. While I did get tearful during the sessions I could not "let go" as I had hoped or as the counselor had hoped. Even in the privacy of a therapist's office, I could not allow myself to break down. I was frustrated that I just could not seem to be honest about sharing my immense grief for fear of losing control. I certainly was not doing myself any favors by suppressing all those feelings. It is still difficult for me but rightly or wrongly it is how I coped with such an unbelievable loss.

Seeing the Accused for the First Time

The arraignment of defendant Kelley was the first time we saw the man accused of murdering our son. A small group of us sat together. Riley and I, along with Steve, several of the bouncers, and Regan's mom, Kathleen, attended that morning. We caught our first real glimpse of Kelley and his girlfriend's aunt, Ms. Wilson. Previously we had only seen what he and Ms. Wilson looked like from the mug shots taken after their arrests. In the large courtroom we were positioned right behind who we believed to be Kelley's father and a woman we assumed was his mother. Riley recalls that the woman wept through the whole arraignment. I do not remember that at all. We saw Kelley's father many times during the course of the trial, but never saw the woman again. I cannot be sure who she was, we never did find out.

Just as it is portrayed on TV, Kelley was in a cage-like holding area in the front of the courtroom. It was off to the right and up from where we sat so it was hard to see him very well, but we got enough of a look at him. I remember being in the courtroom thinking, "this is the man who killed our son." I tried to get the image of him stabbing Brandon out of my mind. As I sat there I thought, "why Brandon, why my son?" Riley was filled with such rage at the sight of Kelley. He had a very hard time staying in his seat and tried to stay composed but wanted more than anything to jump out of his chair.

Kelley didn't look sad or sorry. I suppose I was watching for some sort of remorse, but Kelley just stood there. What was he thinking when he pulled out that knife? Kelley had a criminal record so had been in jail before. In fact, we were told he had a prior record, a felony for assault.

I know now that he couldn't look apologetic or regretful if he was trying to act innocent. He pled not guilty to the charge of murder, attempted murder and assault with a deadly weapon. I thought it was interesting that it was not Kelley who spoke the "not guilty" plea, but those of his counsel. The judge then looked at Kelley and asked if the not guilty plea was correct, to which he answered, yes.

His bail was set at one million dollars. He was held at Orange County Jail in Santa Ana and would remain there until the trial. We were led to believe that he could not afford the 10% bail amount percentage he would be required to pay to secure his release pending the trial. To my knowledge, his portion would have been one hundred thousand dollars.

Ms. Wilson, the woman who knowingly destroyed evidence, was held on fifty thousand dollars bail and also pled not guilty. She was in the courtroom that day in a separate "cage-like" cell. She ultimately served 76 days in the Orange County jail system. Initially she could not post her bail amount percentage either. Bail was eventually lowered enough (to what I do not know) so that she could pay her percentage and she was released pending the trial.

What I found out as time went by was that for Ms. Wilson to be found guilty of accessory to the crime, Kelley would have to be found guilty. It did not make sense to me. If Kelley was found not guilty then that meant, in the eyes of the law, there had been no crime for her to be accessory to.

Nelson, as I mentioned before, was arrested in March 2007 after being indicted by the Grand Jury. He instigated the argument with the bouncers after being removed from the bar. That argument later escalated from who was better the Army or Marines, to the murder of my son and the injury of Steve and Herb. After his indictment and arrest, he was arraigned and pled not guilty. Riley and I were at that arraignment as well. Like his friend Kelley, Nelson's bail was set at one million dollars. He could not make his one hundred thousand dollars bail amount percentage either and remained at Theo Lacy Jail, which is in the city of Orange, until the trial. I believe he had family in the courtroom that day but I could not be sure.

Riley felt that Nelson carried a lot of blame for what happened at the Tavern. Nelson knew what his friend Kelley was capable of yet he kept fueling the argument in the parking lot.

Nelson demeanor was always that of someone who seemed to wonder why he was there, like he was surprised that he might be held accountable for his actions. He never showed any emotion what so ever and never looked at us, not once.

Later, a motion was filed with a request to dismiss all charges. His attorney repeatedly contended that his client had nothing to do with Brandon's murder. The judge denied the motion.

We attended several more pre-trial hearings, motions and requests for continuances. A continuance is a postponement of a date of a trial, hearing or other court appearance. An order for a continuance may be requested from the court by one of the parties, or the parties may agree to a continuance. A continuance may be requested for various reasons, such as unavailability of an attorney or interested party, necessity of extra time to prepare for the matter, and others. We got very tired of hearing that word!

The Long, Long Road to the Trial, and the Love of So Many Along the Way

Let me begin by saying how fortunate we were to have the judge we did. Judge Fasel was present at every hearing, every motion. We were told that he was a very fair judge and a very formal judge. He had presided over many murder and death penalty cases. He was well respected as well as one of the best. We were relieved to know this.

We were encouraged to find out that a "pre-trial" hearing was set for April of 2007. "This was wonderful!" we all thought. The actual trial was to start in late April 2007. Things were moving right along, or so we assumed.

Then we got word that the date was to be moved. Trial dates can be moved or continued for a variety of reasons. In our case there were three defendants, three attorneys, the judge and all their trial schedules. Brahim never seemed surprised that the date moved. I know the attorneys are used to such delays but this was all new to us and it was so disappointing. Why must it take so long?

You hear on the news about trials that take years to get going but we never thought justice for Brandon would take so very long. Of course we were anxious and I asked for the time off from work every time the date changed, only to find out that it was very unlikely that the trial would start. My employers understood that we had no control so I just gave up asking for time off every time the date changed. The first couple of times Riley and I and several others went to the motion hearings. All that happened was that one or the other of the attorneys formally asked the judge to change the date for whatever reason. If we chose not to attend a hearing we would either be contacted by the District Attorneys office or could access the information online through the Superior Court website within hours of the new date being set. All of the trial information is considered public knowledge and, therefore, available to anyone who knows where to look for it. Regan always seemed to have the new court date by retrieving it online before the DA's office even updated us.

Brandon's case was moved to September 2007. That meant several more months of waiting ahead of us. Although we were warned, you truly do not think it will take so long. Our hearts sank at the thought another postponement. There were six continuances in all before the trial actually began. Often it was because one of the attorneys or the judge was still involved in another trial.

The trial was delayed at one point when another case that had also been continued several times, was put ahead of ours because it was a year older. A couple of times the defense asked for more time. We were cautioned that the defense tries to delay things as much as they can. Every time there was a continuance it meant another four to five months more to wait. A new date was scheduled and we did not know until about a week before that it was very unlikely ours would go. In fact, we were told that we might be more surprised when we got the call that the trial was actually going to begin. Again, Brahim never seemed surprised at any of the delays. We never got used to it!

We were warned, "don't put your life on hold." If you want to make vacation plans go ahead and we will work around you. Ok, so we are supposed to say "please move the trial so we can go on vacation!" We did not want to be the cause of any delay so therefore we were afraid to go anywhere, and didn't.

In November 2008, a scary thing happened. Because of a possible conflict of courtrooms and judges, there was a chance that our case would actually start but would be moved to another courtroom and a completely different judge. Our judge had been on this case from the very beginning, every hearing! He knew the case! I began to panic.

We were assured that there were many great judges and we did not doubt that but our judge knew the case and we were very nervous about the possibility of having to change after almost two years. As it turned out (after many, many prayers and me having closed my eyes tight and asking Brandon to help), the decision was made to leave our case in the same courtroom and with Judge Fasel. After a very tense week we were so relieved.

There were many acts of kindness shown to our family during those long months as we awaited the trial. Our friends Joe and Denise planted an oak tree in honor of Brandon. As you may recall, they were two of the friends with us the night Brandon was murdered and with us the next morning at our home.

There is a community park across the street from our house and the tree was planted there at the very edge of the park with a plaque that has Brandon's name on it. A very large and dangerous wild fire threatened our community and the park in October of 2007. We were so worried about all of our homes and that the fire would take Brandon's tree. The tree is still just a baby. The fire went right up to the edge of the park but missed the tree and all of our homes. The tree has new leaves and it currently growing steadily.

Remember Brandon's ring that I cannot bring myself to wash off? A suggestion was made by friend Deb to wash the ring in a bowl of water and use that water to feed Brandon's tree. When I can bring myself to part with the ring, blood and all, that is exactly what we plan to do. As I write this, my eyes are tearful. The tree has such meaning for us and to know that part of Brandon will nourish the tree is such a cool thing. He will live forever in that tree. He was like that tree, tall and strong like an oak.

At a Hennessey's gatherings one of the bouncer's girlfriends asked us to provide her with a couple of pictures of Brandon. Her sister is an artist and wanted to give us a painting of Brandon. We were given a beautiful painting with two different portraits of Brandon's face. We treasure it and it hangs in our bedroom. The artist, Nichole, who I was able to thank personally, said she enjoyed painting it and had Brandon's beautiful smiling face looking at her everyday that she painted it.

My friend Liz gave me a silver pendant in the shape of a teardrop, called "The Memorial Tear." Engraved on the teardrop is a rose and on the back of the pendant is the letter "B". The teardrop symbolizes loss and grief; the rose represents undying love for the one gone but cherished still. I wear it often along with a Celtic cross on the same chain. Liz gave the same pendant to Colleen as well. I treasure it as I treasure our friendship.

At the time of Brandon's death, Steve's girlfriend was a beautiful girl named Lisa. Lisa's is a great cook (especially desserts) and so is her mom Candace. Candace works at a surgery center very close to my office and has told me many times how much she enjoyed having Brandon over to her house and that she "just adored him." Brandon often said how he "loved" Candace's cooking and that she "is the best cook!" Every year on Brandon's birthday Candace and Lisa send me a lovely bouquet of flowers. When Bran's birthday comes around it is such a sad reminder that he is not here with us and the thoughtful flowers make me smile and are so appreciated.

Just a few days after returning to work I got a call from a woman who represented the "Angles of Love." Rick and Sally Cryder founded the Angels of Love. Rick's dream was to create stained glass angels that were freely given to bring encouragement, love, hope, peace and comfort to people during difficult circumstances, whether grieving the loss of a family member or suffering from a serious illness, disability or tragedy.

I was told that an article about Brandon's murder and his dream of becoming a sheriff's deputy seen in the newspaper had prompted the Angels of Love to make an angel in honor of Brandon and present it to me. We learned that many of the angels were given to the families of fallen law enforcement officers and firemen.

Rick Cryder presented our family's angel to me and I was speechless at the gift and cried right there in front of him. Volunteers that donate their time lovingly make each angel. Because Brandon's wish was to become a sheriff's deputy, his angel was made with green stained glass to represent the Orange County Sheriff's department colors. The angel is praying in a kneeling position and there is room for a small tea light candle behind. This angel means so much to our family and is proudly displayed in our home.

We received so so many beautiful and thoughtful cards as well, but there is one I read over and over. I keep it close in a little locked box under my bed, the same locked box that Josh gave me after the fundraisers. Jeremy, a friend of Brandon's from high school sent the card. He was the same age as Brandon but his words had maturity far beyond his years. At the beginning of his card he wrote this:

"It is not only shocking to hear of Brandon's passing, but undoubtedly and painstakingly painful. As a son, brother and young man myself, it is safe to say that we subsume an infallible life; we think we're invincible to action and consequence. I'm sure by now you have heard it a hundred if not a thousand times, but this earth lost a great soul. He had a unique mixture of personality characteristics: he was intimidating, yet approachable; a giant yet gentle; fierce yet admirable; daunting yet courageous; he had the courage and valor of a warrior and the heart of a saint.

I think it is funny that I mention the word warrior now that I think about it. I was reading his My Space about a month ago and somewhere on his page he had a saying on there that eerily characterized his life. He wrote a Viking proverb: "Silent and thoughtful should a warrior be, and bold on the battlefield; cheerful and content should every man be, until he meets his death."

Stumbling around some old college notes of mine I found a quote I written down from a warrior from a different time and place. I immediately thought of Brandon when I read it; it said: "I am ready to meet my Maker. Whether my Maker is prepared for the great ordeal of meeting me is another matter." Even in this time of grief and despair, I couldn't help but utter a chuckle when I put this quote in context to Brandon's life and personality. I do not have a lot of experience with death and I am not sure what more I can do but offer my thoughts and prayers to you and the community who loved and cherished Whitey."

Jeremy went on to quote the poem "For every thing there is a season." To say his card was touching would be an understatement.

Colleen's friend Emily made us a quilt with the words "Blessed are the Peacemakers Matthew 5:9" on it. It is beautiful and it is on display in our den. She also gave us a beautiful silver frame in which we have a picture of Brandon. The frame has a lovely poem engraved on it, part of which I will share.

"Little I knew that morning; God was going to call your name. In life we loved you dearly; in death we do the same. It broke our hearts to lose you; you did not go alone, for part of me went with you the day God called you home." Our family chain is broken and nothing seems the same but as God calls us one by one the chain will link again."

My eyes are wet as I write this (and re-read it). It is hard to read it without emotion and to write of it as well but it means much to us to have it.

One of the most incredible gifts actually came addressed just to me rather than to the family. Inside the package was a small silver jewelry box. The lid was engraved on top, "With Love, John 5:12". Inside the jewelry box I found such an expression of love. Tied in a small pouch was a memory necklace. Actually there were three different sized silver strands of varied lengths, all attached together. The longest length has a small flat silver charm hanging on it with a scripture from the bible, Matthew 5:9 ("Blessed are the Peacemakers") engraved on it. Lying on top of the flat charm hung a beautiful small silver cross. Both of these symbolized Brandon's wish to be a peacemaker and his love of God. The next shortest length held a round brass charm with a Viking ship on it symbolizing Brandon's love for the Nordic part of his heritage. The last and shortest length of the necklace held a small silver locket with a "B" engraved on it. There was a tiny picture of Brandon inside the charm.

Included in the silver box was a hand stamped small book of sorts about two inches tall. Each page of the book held a scripture to match all the charms on the necklace. The last page of the little book said simply "Love, Britney's mom." Also in the pouch was a beautiful delicate beaded necklace with a small square charm that had a "B" on one side and a "W" on the other.

I wore the memory necklace a couple of times but worried I would ruin it so I decided to display it in a long shadow box and included the little hand stamped book open to the Blessed are the Peacemakers page. It hangs right next to my bed and I look at it many times a day. I was so touched by this heartfelt and personal show of kindness and treasure it greatly! The other smaller necklace I wear often and treasure it as well.

There was one final note in the box. An address was included in case I wanted a different picture in the locket. The note said that her prayers were with me and it was signed "Love, a mom." From one mom to another, an act of caring that I will never forget.

There were many, including the four of us, who called Brandon's cell phone just to hear his voice. After several months the time came to turn it off. Riley wanted to keep the phone on so long as there were people still calling it. I feared the loss of his voice on the voice mail. To never get to hear that deep voice say "this is Brandon White, leave a message" again, even as a recording, made me so sad. My friend Don is a wonderful man as well as a computer wiz. He was able to record Brandon's voice mail message onto a disk for me. I will have it always and can listen to it when I am particularly down, you know those times when you just need to hear someone's voice.

About a month after the funeral, we hosted the first "bouncer BBQ" as we called them. They were a gathering of Brandon's closest friends here at our home. We felt closer to Brandon with the kids here and they felt closer to him by being with us. We learned so much about Brandon from all the kids. I think your friends see a side of you that your parents don't and it was fun to hear their stories about Brandon that he would not have necessarily have told us himself. Melissa and Molly, who are two of Brandon's friends and also girlfriends to two of his closest friends, were instrumental in organizing and inviting those who attended the BBQ's.

I am honored to call these women my friends as well. It has been such a joy to get to know them. Molly and Brandon were very close and among other things shared the same beautiful hair. Melissa, also a red head, is quite the cook and her desserts are very much looked forward too. Melissa also did Colleen's makeup for her Senior Prom. Another event she was sad her brother did not get to see her attend.

We had the BBQ's every month for the first year, usually the last Sunday of the month. The BBQ's were and are a potluck of sorts and we were never sure what everyone would bring. One Sunday one of the boys brought live lobsters. I could not watch as the lobsters were put in the pot to cook. Josh often makes his famous chicken enchiladas or we just have hamburgers. All the girls, including good friend Becky, who has also been so supportive in so many ways, help clean up. We play beer pong or just all hang out and talk. Now we get together every few months.

Brandon's friends are very wonderful people and it is a real testimony to him to have had such considerate and devoted friends who loved him so much. It was so amazing to see Brandon through their eyes. To them he was almost bigger than life. They loved him, respected him and miss him so much.

One of the most difficult things I experienced through all of this was the hideous blogs on the Internet. There was a "forum" (or discussion) on line where the incident at the Tavern was discussed. I think the blogs are started by a website that takes topics from the news headlines. People can write in and converse about or debate over any given current event or subject.

I was inadvertently told of the blog and never should have looked at it. I came to regret it. Neither Riley nor Sean ever looked at it, refused to as a matter of fact, and were mad at me for doing so. If any of Brandon's friends knew about it they never talked of it in my presence. Colleen had no idea about the blog and for that I was grateful.

Horrible things were said about our son and what happened that night. We can only assume those involved with or known by the defendants wrote the untrue statements. You are only identified by a screen name on the forum. Unless you choose to divulge your true name, we will never know for sure who wrote on the forum. Things like, "I am glad he's dead", "How funny it was to see all that blood come out of his neck", "He got what he deserved", "He was guilty of his own demise" and that he "was in hell." Numerous heinous and hurtful comments and responses to those statements were added over the months before the trial.

Others who also read the blogs made complaints to the organizers of the forum. Statements made in such poor taste were removed and that person banned from writing. Sadly someone who just changed his or her screen name and wrote again would replace previous comments with more upsetting ones.

I wanted to scream at those who were writing such awful things, anxious to write back and defend my son. I wanted to say, "I am his mom and how dare you!" among other things (I am holding myself back in my description of what I really wanted to say). I had made several promises not to get involved, and never did. I never wanted anyone to accuse me of acting inappropriately and I certainly did not want to do anything to jeopardize the case. It was very, very, very difficult to stay silent.

There were, of course, many encouraging responses to the awful things written about Brandon and the others who were involved that night. Again, since you do not know who is writing on the forum I do not know who responded on Brandon's behalf. I have to admit I was always very happy to read a positive, true statement.

It got very ugly for a while. I sat at the computer and cried alone while reading the lies and untruths. Those who were writing could not possibly know my son so why would they write such falsehoods. I was so livid and frustrated that there was nothing I could do to stop it.

Due to freedom of speech, not much of anything could be done about the inexcusable words written. I am not proud about getting caught up in the whole thing. I tried to tell myself that I wanted to read everything I could to prepare myself for the upcoming trial. I did not want to be surprised by anything the defense tried to say about Brandon.

The truth is, it was sort of an addiction at the time. Not a healthy place for me to be at all! I hoped that if no one responded to these people, after a while they would get tired of writing. I finally stopped looking at the forum. The truth would come out at the trial and there would no longer be anything they could say. I would encourage anyone to avoid those forums and getting caught up in the comments. Nothing good can come of it.

I was told that those who were writing such monstrous things were trying to "get a rise" out of whomever was reading it. What kind of people were these? There was no compassion for the pain and sadness from the loss of a life. I would like to say something to all those who wrote those appalling comments. "Your actions in writing on that blog were pitiful. The hand of your friend murdered our son. All you accomplished was to leave a mother mourning the tragic loss of her son, heartsick, depressed and troubled. You are pathetic and I hope you all feel ashamed. Sadly, I fear this is not the case and I feel sorry for you all."

Our Way to Memorialize Brandon

In April of 2007 I had a portrait tattoo of Brandon done. Getting a tattoo seemed a natural and permanent way for me to honor my son.

I got my first tattoo four years ago at the age of 46. Obviously getting a tattoo was something I had thought about for quite some time before actually doing it. I did not consider myself a "tattoo person" at first, but thought they were cool on other people.

My first tattoo, a fairy (with red hair of course) was done on my lower back. With three red headed children, the fairy had to have red hair. Rob, the artist, had tattooed both my boys and that was how we met. It seemed only fitting that he do my very first tattoo as well. The fairy, wrapped only in a vine, has her red hair flowing around her. Her wings are beautiful and colorful.

Getting a tattoo hurt (Rob said it was "a rite of passage") and I vowed that day, never to get another. Rob smiled and waved an imaginary wand in the air and said something I will never forget; "you'll be back."

Right after getting a tattoo it feels similar to being sunburned for a day or two and then gets really itchy and peels. Once it heals though, it looks great! I soon forgot about any discomfort and yes, I did go back. Later I got a small red rose on my back by my left shoulder. I thought that it would be the only tattoo I ever had there. Following Brandon's death I wanted a remembrance of him that only I would have. My back seemed an obvious and perfect spot.

Brandon and Regan had gone to a black tie event about two weeks before he was killed. He had been invited to the five-year anniversary of the St. Regis Hotel in Dana Point. The St. Regis is a four star, well known hotel in the area. Brandon had opportunity to meet the owner of the hotel and was offered an invitation to the celebration. Brandon picked up Regan at her apartment and several pictures were taken of the pair in their formal wear. A couple of pictures were taken of just Brandon. I loved Brandon's smile in those pictures, he looked so happy. I chose a picture from that night as the perfect tattoo.

I asked Franco if he would do the tattoo of Brandon. Franco is well known in the tattoo world for his artwork and his portrait tattoos. He also owned the tattoo shop in Orange County where Rob works. Franco was honored to do the tattoo and since he knew Brandon it made it all the more special for the both of us. I have learned that when a tattoo is so meaningful to the person getting it, the artist finds it meaningful as well. Franco's portrait of Brandon was incredible! The tattoo is just of his head and neck. Franco made it look as if he is coming out of the clouds. Below the tattoo he freehanded and tattooed the words "Blessed are the Peacemakers." He captured Brandon's essence and his eyes seem to sparkle and look right at you. I treasure the tattoo and Brandon will forever "have my back!"

Later I added a white rose to the other rose on my back to symbolize the "white rose of truth." You will read about the meaning behind that and the inspiration for my book title later.

Riley and Sean and many of Brandon's friends also got memorial tattoos. Some, including Riley got a Celtic cross similar to a tattoo Brandon had. Riley had his placed over his heart. Regan had a Celtic cross tattooed in the middle of her back and another friend put her memorial cross tattoo on her ankle. Sean and some of the guys got a skull from a favorite print Brandon had. The artist, Andy is a friend of mine and I know he will be famous someday! Sean and Bran had several of Andy's works in their room but especially loved the skull drawing.

Colleen had to wait until she was 18 for her memorial tattoo. She had her own idea of how she chose to remember her brother. She wanted Brandon's signature in a tattoo. Rob took Brandon's first name from his driver's license signature and his last name from the signature on his social security card. That combination was the clearest representation. Now Colleen forever has Brandon's signature on the top of her foot, outlined with a heart and his date of birth and date of death.

People get tattoos for a variety of reasons but for all of us the memorial tattoos were for a very emotional and for me spiritual reason. To have them done by artists that knew our son was so special to all of us.

How Do I Act?

When you meet new people, an obvious question is "how many children do you have?" I found this a very complicated question to answer. Of course I have three children, Sean, Brandon and Colleen. The uncomfortable part was how to say that I had three children and now one was gone. It is difficult to bring up the story of his murder when you have just met someone or are seeing someone you have not seen for a long time.

I have always been a friendly person and still consider myself as such. I find that I hold back a bit more now in a big group, especially if there are many I do not know. I tend to gravitate towards the people I do know. This is another example of how Brandon's murder has changed me. I hesitate in initiating conversation. That is not to say that I do not have many things to share about Sean and Colleen, because I do. They have many exciting events happening in their lives that I love to boast about.

An example of this discomfort in bringing up Brandon's murder was my 30th high school reunion in August of 2007. I hesitated in even going because I felt I would not know what to say. It was only eight months after Brandon's death.

Two of my very close friends, Mary, who has been my friend since grade school, and Ginelle, who I have known since my freshman year of high school, urged me to go and promised they would stick by me. Interestingly Mary and I, besides sharing a long time friendship, both have three children, two boys and a girl. In fact, our boys are the exact same ages. Colleen and Mary's daughter are only a year apart with Colleen being older.

After much debate I agreed to go. It was just as I feared. I was very uncomfortable and just stood there and smiled as everyone talked about all the wonderful things their kids were doing. I pretended that I had three live children that night, just because it was easier. I told of their ages and where they were going to school and what they were doing.

I did take a couple of my closest high school friends aside and told them of what had happened to Brandon. Of course they were sorry but I know it must have been rough for them not knowing what to say to me other than they were sorry. It is a common thing; no one knows what to say to someone who has lost a child.

I felt bad that Mary and Ginelle were stuck hanging out with me when they both found former classmates they wanted to spend time catching up with. Sweet Riley came and picked me up early and I was so grateful and so ready to leave. It was not an easy evening for me and looking back I think just a bit too early for me to have been in such a large group.

Sadly, three months later, on November 1st, 2007, Mary's middle child Scotty who was also 21 at the time, committed suicide. He was an outgoing, seemingly happy boy from a wonderful, close family. His mom describes him as a "sweet sensitive soul." He silently had battled depression and felt for whatever reason he could not go on. At his funeral, a video of Scotty and his friends was shown. How could this fun loving boy in the video, so full of joy and promise, end his own life? These are questions his family still asks.

I will never forget what Mary wrote to me in one of our many correspondences; "Who would have ever thought we would have had this to share?" They had lost their beloved boy and their hearts were broken.

She now understood how I felt. I do not wish this understanding on another human being. Until you have experienced such a loss, no one can understand the depth of the sadness. You do not want ANYONE to understand, really. It is very hard to explain. There can be sympathy and those who share your sadness. It is difficult to truly fathom the void in your life that losing a child opens. A void that I fear time will never fill.

I recently attended the wedding of a co-worker and was introduced to one of her friends who asked me the dreaded question. "So how old are your children?" This time I told her only of Sean and Colleen. As you stand there, you must to think fast about what to say. I was thinking that she must have wondered about the big gap in the kid's ages but she didn't say anything. Nine years separate Sean and Colleen.

As I spoke to her I felt I was being untruthful not bringing up Brandon. A wedding is such a happy occasion and not the place to talk of his death or explain what happened to him so I stood there and smiled and felt uncomfortable.

My hope is that one-day I will feel comfortable in my responses to such questions. As time has gone by, and I meet new people or see old friends, I tell them I have three children, two living and one in heaven. I have found that this is an easier way to handle it. I think it just took time for me to work it out in my head and feel at ease with my response.

To Dream Or Not to Dream

I was always sure I would see Brandon again in my dreams. Dreaming of him seemed to elude me. It was Riley who dreamt of him first, but not for about three months after his death.

In Riley's dream, Brandon was standing outside a set of double doors. Riley did not know where the doors were located. Brandon was wearing a pair of shorts, a light blue shirt and his rainbow sandals. Riley remembers that many people were filing through the doors. Brandon did not see his dad right away. He just kept beckoning everyone to "just keep moving forward." Brandon was smiling and seemed happy as were all those who were going through the doors. Then, Riley says, Brandon glanced over at him and said, " It's ok." At that point Riley woke up (reluctantly). He wanted to keep dreaming of seeing Brandon.

He did not dream of Brandon again for a year after that. This time the dream took place in a big room where a party or reception was going on. Riley saw him and said, "Bran", calling out to get his attention. Brandon came over to his dad and with a big smile on his face, gave Riley a hug. He said, "I'm ok" to his dad. Riley turned around to see if I was there so he could call me over. When he turned back around, Brandon was gone. It was then that Riley woke up.

The last time Riley dreamt of Brandon was more recently. Sean was also in his dream this time. He and Brandon were much younger, maybe ages ten and seven. The boys were with their dad on a small sailboat that Riley owned before we started dating. The three of them were sailing on Mission Bay in San Diego, a favorite location of Riley's. The boys were laughing and Brandon was dragging his hand through the water. In the dream Riley recalls how vividly red their hair was in the sun. He says at that point, I woke him up (sorry Riley!).

I am sad to say that I have only dreamt of Brandon once. It was not until a year after he was murdered. I was in a room filled with many people (seems to be a common dream) and saw Brandon across the room. I tried to get to him but I could not seem to move. I could not reach him and remember feeling frustrated in my dream. I know he saw me but Brandon did not speak to me as he had in his dads dream. I woke up then with such a feeling of joy at having seen him but also with sadness that it was only a dream. I long to see his face, hear his voice and hope more dreams will come.

Colleen says she has not dreamt of her brother yet and Sean says he has a few times, but wakes up and cannot recall the dream. I hate when that happens and we all know it does with some dreams that you really would like to remember. Sean says from what he can remember, his dreams are about he and his brother hanging out with friends but that is all he can bring to mind.

My sister-in-law, Cindy (Riley's sister), recently told me about a dream she had about Brandon. She hesitated to tell me about it for fear it would make me sad but in actuality her story warmed my heart.

She started out by saying that her dream occurred one Sunday morning when she and David were able to sleep in. She thinks the dream took place in their bedroom.

She heard a voice that she immediately recognized as Brandon's say, "Aunt Cindy?" She replied, "Brandon?" He then said," Aunt Cindy, its me Brandon, you are not doing your job!" In the dream Cindy remembered thinking, "What job am I not doing?" "I know it's hard," he continued, "but you have to tell her." "Tell my mom I'm ok and that I am happy." Cindy asked him how she was supposed to make me believe her. He said, "Tell her that I hate peas (Brandon hated peas) and she will know, and Aunt Cindy, tell her one more thing. Tell her to tell Sean that I am beside him always." She said that's when she woke up and remembers such a feeling of peace at having seen Brandon.

I am so glad Cindy was able to recall the dream so she could share it with me. I want to believe with all my heart that Brandon is all right and that he came to Cindy in her dreams to make sure I knew that.

What's In a Word?

There are words and phrases I would love to have stricken from the dictionary. Words like "closure" "move on, "getting over" and "healing." These are words that are used by well meaning people but often make me wince when I hear them used in reference to our son's murder.

For me, I fear there will never be "closure". That is why I don't like the word. Closure to me means end, conclusion or finality. It is just not a word I can relate to at this point. The people that care about you want you to have a conclusion or closure. They want you to be OK, to be better. If you admit that yes, you have closure, then they don't have to be so worried about you. At least that is what I tell myself. Could anyone use that word in reference to himself or herself after an experience such as ours?

I feel like our family is sort of "stuck in grief." All around us the world is turning, our friends and family's lives are continuing to "move on" but ours is not, at least not at the pace of everyone else's. I know many of Brandon's friends grieve deeply for him to this day. How long can you expect everyone to grieve at the same level and for as long as you are? Grief is a very personal thing and cannot be measured in time and space.

Another phrase that gets to me is "he's in a better place." One more well meant statement that makes me flinch and I am never quite sure how to respond to. The place I want Brandon to be is here with me. Do I believe Brandon is in heaven, absolutely! Am I being selfish, maybe? Then there is the ever popular "it was meant to be." People have actually said this to me. I myself have used that very phrase when explaining how an item I wanted to buy and didn't, was still there when I went back to the store. It was "meant to be." or "it was fate." However, in relating that phrase to Brandon, how can the murder of a great young man, full of promise be "meant to be?"

I think that sometimes it must be uncomfortable to be around us. There are those who do not know what to say or how to act. My cousin wrote to me and explained that she just didn't know how to communicate with people who had experienced a loss and felt bad for not being supportive. It didn't mean that she wasn't caring and I appreciated her candor. She was, by no means, unsympathetic, but like many could not verbalize it.

To be honest, I feel better when I talk about Brandon, mostly with people who already know what happened. He is never far from my thoughts so I enjoy talking about him and get comfort from it. There are those who do not really bring him up when we are together and I am not sure if they think we need a break from thinking about him or that they are uncomfortable with the subject. It could be some of both.

There is always a part of me that is a little bit sad. Sure I have fun and go out but there is always a little black cloud over everything I do. Some are more in tune with my feelings than others. I certainly hope I do not come across as a downer all the time. I have had to cut my self some slack about that. I am most comfortable with those who don't mind talking about Brandon. Again, to really understand the need to talk of him, one must have an understanding of the depth of loss, and understanding that a part of my heart is missing. It is a club I wish no one to join.

I think I am a fun and friendly person. Our son was taken from us and in a violent way. We are not the same people we were before. Those closest to us get that and I have to hope that as time passes the hurt will soften.

A good friend told me that maybe it was time to think about celebrating Brandon's life. She was referring to my hesitancy in watching the slide presentation that was shown at the funeral. Her words were from love and not intended to wound me. I told her it would make me sad to see the slide show again in its entirety. She wondered if she had crossed a line in saying what she did. I didn't feel that way at all and appreciated the honesty in her words.

I think in many ways we have celebrated his life. Every time I look at one of the thoughtful gifts we were given, the drawing on the napkin or the memory necklace or the painting of Brandon just to name a few, I do celebrate his life. I get such a warm feeling when I see these things.

The scholarship fund, to me is a celebration of his life. To be able to give back to the sport and the school that Bran loved so much, celebrates his life and his love of football.

I think that when you are personally in the midst of an overwhelming sense of loss, especially that of a child, celebration of that life gets lost in your heavy heartedness. Having said that, I do think that there is more than one definition of celebration. To me, to celebrate is to rejoice. After some thought, to celebrate can also mean to honor and I certainly feel I have done that. Thank you Michelle, my dear friend your words have given me lots to think about!

Pictures to Share

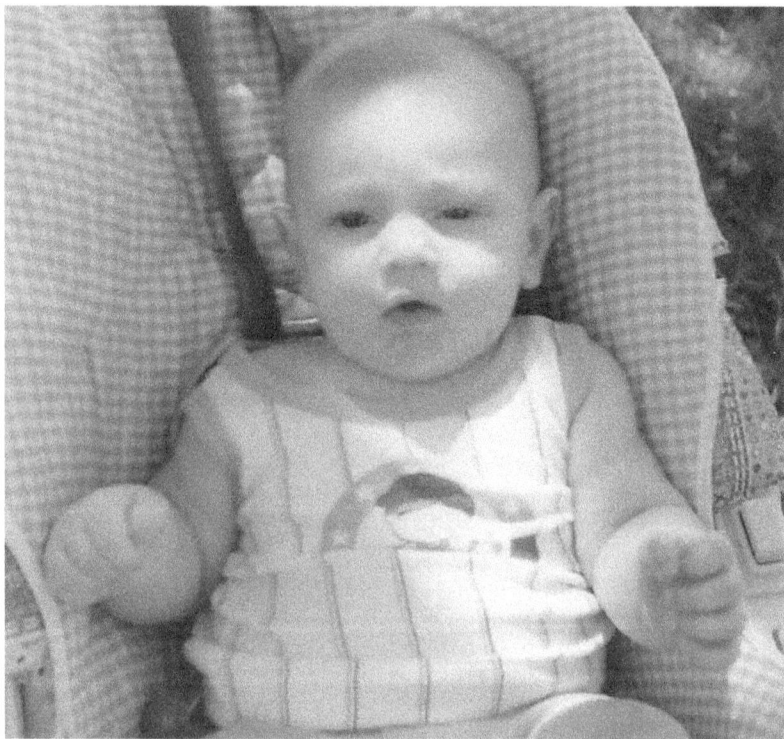

Baby Brandon, 2 months old, July 1985

Sean age 6, Brandon age 2

Brandon, age 5, with newborn Colleen

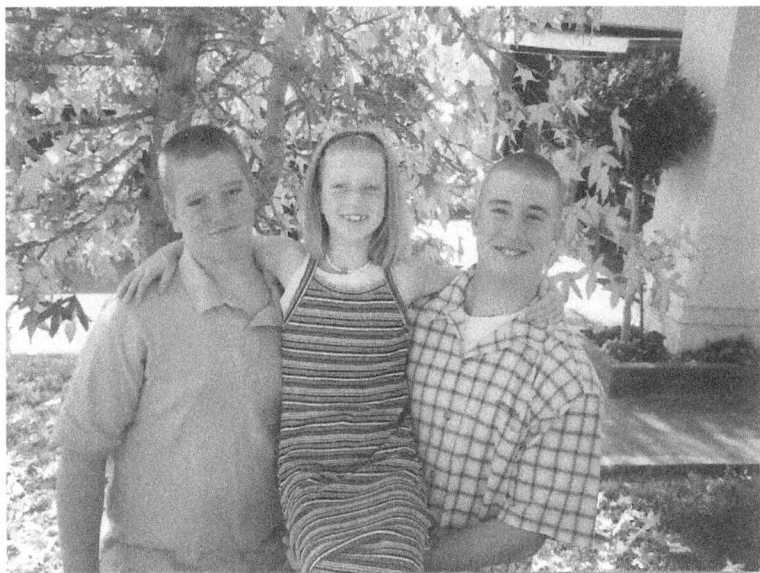

Sean 16, Bran 13, Colleen 8, 1998

Brandon and Sean, 2000

Riley, Bran and Erin, during Brandon's time
playing football at Saddleback Community College,2005.

Brandon and I, on San Clemente Pier

Brandon and Sean in Viking helmets,
Las Vegas, 2006

Blake, Steve and Brandon in back, Brian in front, at high school
graduation

Brian, Blake, Steve and Brandon, 2006

Molly and "B"

Herb and Brandon

Herb and Patrick (Pat) in back, Mark and Brandon in front

Melissa and Erin

Brandon and Josh

Brandon and Regan, December 2006

Jerod and Cassie

My friend Deb photo shopped Colleen in after she got her first tattoo in 2008. All tattoo's by Rob.
Original photo taken 2006

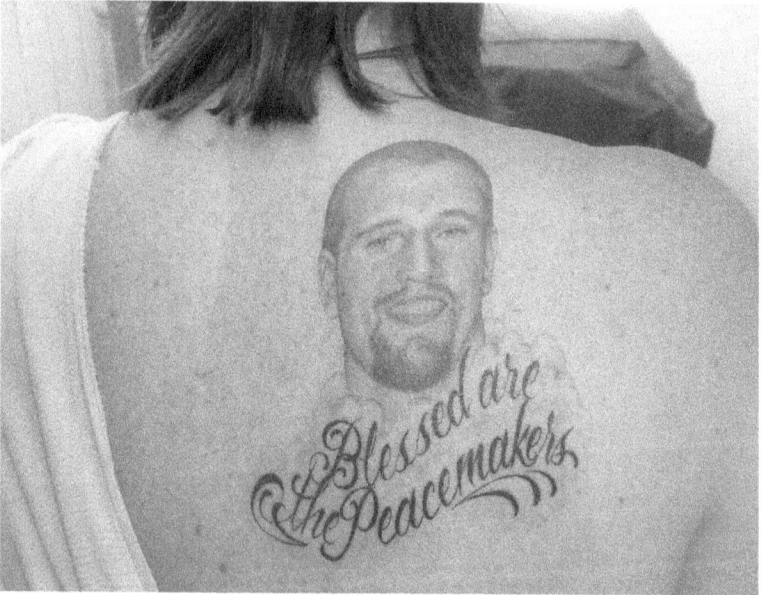

My portrait tattoo of Brandon, 2007

The Trial... At Last!

Finally, after many frustrations, delays, hearings, motions and continuances, the trial was set to commence. One year, eleven months and two days had passed since Brandon's murder. At last we were hopeful that justice would be served for him and for Steve. Brahim had been exactly right in his prediction that the trial might take two years to start.

Jury selection was scheduled to begin on December 2, 2008. Selection of a jury can be a long process and we were told that the estimate for our case was about one full day. That meant that the actual trial was scheduled to start on December 3rd.

We were notified that the family could be present during jury selection but that it was possible we might be seated next to a prospective juror during the process since everyone assembles in the same room. After some discussion, we felt that it was not appropriate that we be there. I think it would have been an interesting experience but the decision was made as a family that we would not attend.

The morning of December 3rd while I was getting dressed for court Riley went out to get the newspaper. On the doorstep was a small package that must have been delivered late and missed the night before. The package was addressed to me. Inside the padded envelope, a note and a gift from Donna, who is my brother-in-law David's sister. I have known Donna for over thirty years. Donna works in a hospital and has been a nurse for many years. She wrote that she never goes into the gift shop at the hospital but for some reason stopped in, saw a bracelet and thought of me. It was a beautiful Marquisate bracelet with an angel attached. I was so thrilled.

I was feeling so very nervous about the days to come and believed it was actually fortunate that the package had been missed the prior night because it was the perfect gift and came on the perfect day at the perfect time. I wore the bracelet that day and every day we were in court. I felt it must be a good luck charm. I could not thank Donna enough for thinking of me and her gift meant so very much.

We were told to arrive at the courthouse by 9:00 a.m. and advised everyone who planned on attending to first come to the cafeteria on the third floor of the courthouse. The cafeteria became our meeting place every day. It was a very spacious room with a multitude of large tables and many chairs. In the Superior Courthouse in Santa Ana, the cafeteria is right next to a massive room where prospective jurors gather to wait during jury duty. An outside patio was easily accessible for those who might need some air.

The cafeteria was a busy place. At anytime there could be jurors or prospective jurors taking a break or families like us waiting for court to begin. Relatives might pass the time there hoping for verdicts to be decided or plaintiffs with minor offences anticipating their day in court. It is also a convenient area where some attorneys met clients to discuss options before a case was heard.

Next to the cafeteria is a place one can buy a hot meal, prepackaged foods, an array of chips, cookies, mints or the like. Cold beverages and coffee are also available. I have to say, over all, the food was not half bad. We also got the inside scoop on a great deli within walking distance of the courthouse and spent many a lunch hour there as a group.

We were fortunate to have the support of many family and friends with us that day. The first day of a trial typically begins with opening statements by both the prosecution and the defense. Brahim told us the opening and closing statements were the most important and if anyone wanted to join us, those were the best days.

Riley and I expected that there would be many present on those particular days and wondered if we would be sitting alone in the courtroom on all the others. It was Christmas time, folks were busy or needed to work so we weren't sure who all would attend. As it turned out, we were NEVER alone and in fact were amazed at how many people representing our family made the effort to come. Riley, Sean, Colleen and I were so thankful for that.

As we sat in the cafeteria that morning waiting to be called into the courtroom, it became apparent that nothing was going to start on time. Nine o'clock had come and gone with no summons to the courtroom. What could be going on? Our victim's assistant stopped by around 10:00 a.m. and informed us that jury selection had not been completed the day before and was currently still in process. We continued to wait, hoping to get word. By lunchtime we were informed that jury selection would not be completed in time and that the trial would not start until the following day. It seemed there was no need for us to wait any longer. My shoulders drooped in disappointment at the thought of another delay.

There are offices on the second floor of the courthouse that the DA's utilize during trials. Brahim asked to meet with all of us in a private conference room adjacent to those offices before we went home. He discussed with us what was to happen in the coming days and answered questions from the group as well. We ended up meeting with him several times during the course of the trial.

During our time with Brahim we were also clued-in to why there had been a delay in jury selection. A prospective juror had had a seizure in the courtroom the day before and that delayed the process by about three hours. Then later on during the selection a woman broke down in the jury box while being questioned. It turned out that she knew Brandon personally. I believe that the prospective jurors were told that this was a murder trial but initially not told for whom. She had no idea it was Brandon's.

At some point it must have been made known that the trial was for Brandon's murder. She broke down sobbing and was excused by the judge. I have never been told who she was. I felt really terrible about what happened and that she had such an emotional experience. I can only hope that maybe someday she will read this book and know how very sorry I am for what she went through.

Prospective jurors are selected randomly to be in the "jury box" and are then questioned by both the defense and prosecuting attorneys. There are fourteen spots, twelve actual jurors and two alternate jurors who attend everyday just as the twelve do. If for any reason one of the jurors cannot perform their duty, they can be excused by the judge and alternate sworn in. A juror is not excused lightly, however.

I always knew that the attorneys could excuse a certain amount of prospective jurors during the selection process. What I didn't know was there really is no limit to how many can be excused, if there is good reason. No wonder jury selections can take so long!

Shortly after meeting with Brahim, we thanked everyone for coming and went home. By 5:00 p.m. we had received a call and were told that jury selection was completed and the opening statements would be the following morning at 9:00 a.m.

Later that evening, I sat down at the computer to let as many people as I could know what had happened. Only those who were there knew that opening statements had not occurred. I figured emailing everyone would save me from a lot of phone calls. I could have been on the phone all night trying to contact everyone.

There were so many who wanted to be kept in the loop so I created a "group" email. It started out as just a way to get the word out most efficiently. The group list grew every day. Along with the text messages all the kids sent to each other with updates, we were able to have quite an information network. The ability to text as a quick way to communicate will become very important later.

I think that the positive feedback I received about the emails was yet another reason I decided to put my experiences on paper. Coming home and emailing the day's events also helped me keep everything straight in my mind. Many told me that although they could not be in the courtroom with us, they felt like they were actually there while reading my description of the day's proceedings.

As I stated earlier, when I first began writing about the night at the Tavern, I decided that I did not want to give names to the men responsible. Calling them defendant 1 and defendant 2 got very confusing for me while I wrote and I was sure, equally as confusing to anyone who might be reading it. Still I continued on with my chosen way of reference. I was positive I did not want to use their names; sure they did not deserve it.

After the decision to include my daily emails as part of the story I decided it just didn't make sense not to use the defendants names. When writing to family I certainly would not refer to them as defendant 1 and 2. Their names were public record so before I got too far I decided to go back and change my references regarding them and used their last names only. It was either that or exclude my emails altogether. I really felt these communications were important to the story; important not only because of the content but because everyone would really get a true sense of how we felt and what transpired every day.

We had been told that our behavior and that of anyone who attended the trial on our family's behalf was of utmost importance. We were all there to represent Brandon. We were advised not to react negatively or be overly emotional while in court. The jury sees "everything" they said. This could prove to be a difficult task, I thought. Emotions run very high during an event like this. Our whole family was emotional; all of Brandon's friends were emotional. I was extremely nervous about what was to happen, the process of the trial, and the outcome. What if the verdict was not what we hoped for? What then?

When we were not in the courtroom we were advised not to talk of what went on in that room. That meant when we were at the courthouse we could not discuss with each other or anyone what had occurred. We had to be careful in the bathroom, in the cafeteria and especially in the elevators. The elevators were usually packed (like sardines) full of people.

Court usually started at 9:00 a.m. everyday except Friday. That day was reserved for smaller cases lasting a day or less. The judge usually called a break at around 10:30 a.m., then lunch from about noon or so until 1:30 p.m., then another break at 3:00 p.m. Depending on the day and who was testifying court adjourned anywhere between 4:00 p.m. and 5:00 p.m.

That meant that there could several times during the day that we all might be standing out side the courtroom. However, also standing outside the courtroom were friends and family of the defendants, the jurors and possibly an attorney or two. There was a small group of family and friends for the defendants that attended regularly. We mostly knew who they were but those attending the trial for either side could change daily.

When it was likely the trial would begin, I was sent the court instructions from our victim's assistant. I passed on the email to everyone we thought might attend. I personally met with or had a conversation with all the kids. By kids, I mean my two children and all of their friends and Brandon's friends. I truly feel that all of my children's friends are like family. These "kids" are actually adults but they are still kids to me. I tried to convey the importance of how they dressed and how they behaved and its impact on the trial. Our BBQ's were a great way to talk to them as a group.

I believe now that I really never needed to tell them how to act. I am so proud of ALL of them. Everyone conducted themselves perfectly. Riley and I could not have asked for more. Some actually came to court in suits, or they were dressed very nicely. There was never one bit of trouble from anyone who attended on our behalf.

Our victim's assistant Melissa was asked by an investigator who had attended the trial if she was nervous about being in charge of crowd control for such a large group. She answered quickly "Absolutely not!" Her words were a wonderful testimony to our group, their love for us, and for Brandon!

On any given day there were at least 15 to 50 or more people there to support us and represent Brandon. Knowing there was so much love in the courtroom for us meant more than I can put into words. The affection they all had for Bran and for us was like big arms that wrapped around us and made us stronger.

My sister Maureen and her husband Brian were frequent attendants as well as my sister Sheila, my brother Kevin, his wife Dianna and son Craig. Pastor Greg and his associate Mary also attended often. In fact, Pastor Greg led us all in prayer on the opening statement day. It was a very profound experience as we all prayed together.

My girlfriends Kelly and Tracy from down south and up north made the drive to lend their support. Regan, Brandon's girlfriend had moved to New York about a year after Brandon's death but flew in part of the time and Regan's mom Kathleen was there everyday with us. My good friend Deb and our mutual friend Suzanne supported us as often as they could. Suzanne often sat in the back of the middle section and observed the jury, letting us know that they always seemed attentive and focused. From our seats we were very close to the jury but sat to the side of them so actually seeing their faces was difficult. It was helpful to see them from Suzanne's perspective.

Many of Brandon's friends and fellow bouncers were also with us most days. Patrick and Molly, Jerod and Cassie and Big Joe were with us commonly. Herb's mom Laura was there many days and Herb's girlfriend Melissa missed as much work as she could to be there. Steve's dad also attended. Since Brandon and Steve had so many mutual friends, there was support from all over to sustain us and stand behind us through the long days. Sean and Colleen also had friends that attended on their behalf.

I got so nervous every day that my "potty" breaks became somewhat of a source of amusement among our crowd. I probably took a couple of trips to the bathroom, which was right outside the door, before the court was brought to order. If the judge was delayed at all I was sneaking out the door before things got started. Our family sat in the same place every day, which was very close to the front, and I had to walk by everyone on the way out and hear them say, "You are going AGAIN!" My constant bathroom breaks could have also been all the coffee and diet Coke I consumed too, I guess.

Speaking of the judge, Judge Fasel is well known in Orange County. As I stated earlier he is a very formal judge and also known as a fair judge. There were rules of his courtroom posted outside the door that included no food, gum or drinks in his courtroom. No one said anything to me about my sneaking a sip from a water bottle (hidden in my purse) or having an occasional mint, however.

Judge Fasel did not tolerate misbehavior in his courtroom. Early on in the trial one of the defendant's friends or family, I do not know which; actually fell asleep in his chair. Soon there was a note from the judge handed to the bailiff. The bailiff motioned to the person sitting next to the sleeping man to "wake him up!" I saw all of this because from where I sat I could see the bailiff at all times. Next thing I knew the bailiff walked over to the man and escorted him out. I did not see that man again so I am not sure he ever came back.

I had never been to an actual trial before. I'd had jury duty many times and gotten close but had never actually been involved in a trial. It was interesting to see that on the judges desk, just to the right of him, was a computer monitor. If counsel for the defense or the prosecution objected to something that was said, Judge Fasel referred to that screen and read what the court reporter had entered before making the decision to overrule or sustain the objection.

There was always a large sheriff presence in the courtroom. Besides the bailiffs who were the same men everyday, each of the defendants had a sheriff's deputy in attendance at all times. Another deputy was always posted just inside the door. On any given day we might see even more than the usual deputies throughout the courtroom.

One of the bailiffs opened the door around 9 a.m. and those of us in attendance, including the defendant's supporters, filed into the courtroom and were seated. We all usually sat in pretty much the same spots. Our family and friends sat on the far left of the large courtroom as you faced the judge. The jury could see us very easily if they just turned their heads to the right. Our courtroom, we learned, was one of the largest and we were happy about that for a couple of reasons. For one thing there were over 200 seats in this particular courtroom. Not all of the courtrooms were that big so that meant plenty of seating. Another plus was a very large window along our side of the room. The window added light and was a welcome addition to such formal surroundings.

We were seated very close to Brahim and Joe Gaul. The bailiffs asked that the first couple of rows of our section remain empty. Those rows were very close to the jury so I figured that was why they didn't want us up that far. Riley, Sean, Colleen and I were in the front just about twelve feet behind Brahim and Joe, separated by a railing. The two of them sat at a very long table together that faced the judge. Brahim was on the far left end, then Joe right next to him. Next to Joe, at an adjacent table was Nelson's attorney, then Nelson. Next to Nelson, Kelley and his attorney sat on the far right end.

The defendant's supporters sat mostly in the middle section of the room behind Kelley and Nelson. I believe they were a mix of family and friends. There were those that we saw most every day and some we only saw once or twice.

Counsel was always in the room when we arrived, along with the court reporter that typed the transcripts of all conversations and the secretary who, among other things, swore in whomever was testifying. All three of the attorneys had three-tiered, rolling file carts of all the interviews, reports and testimonies. Huge file holders took up every tier. The attorneys often referred to these files during the day so I assumed that they were similar if not the same. It amazed all of us that Brahim might ask to reference page 1512, for example, and knew exactly what he was looking for. The rolling carts reminded me of the ones you see library employees push around the library while returning books to the correct spot. None of these files were ever left in the courtroom when it was empty. I saw all three attorneys personally rolling their carts out of the courtroom at the end of the day. I noticed Kelley's attorney pushing hers out of the building one evening. I wondered if her office was close by or if all the files went into her car.

Brahim had a lap top computer that he used daily. In court he used it mostly for viewing pictures or videos that were projected onto a big screen suspended above the courtroom.

Brahim informed us early on that both men accused had public defenders. The court appoints a public defender for those who cannot, for whatever reason, provide their own counsel. This is often due to cost.

Brahim told us that he had been in court cases with both public defenders and that we might see all of them conversing in a social manner. He wanted to assure us that "nothing would take away the severity of this trial" but that they all knew each other and might have a friendly exchange prior to starting the day, which they often did. He told us that both of the defense attorneys were very good. Kelley's counsel was female and Nelson's male.

Nelson was brought into the courtroom first accompanied by a sheriff's deputy and always handcuffed behind his back. He was transported from Theo Lacy jail and held in a room on a lower level of the courthouse and escorted up. He strolled into the courtroom and did not really look at anyone during the short walk to his seat. He placed his arms over the back of the chair and the sheriff's deputy uncuffed him. He and his attorney then spoke quietly. Nelson wore slacks and a dress shirt but no tie that I recall.

Kelley was brought in after Nelson, un-handcuffed. A sheriff's deputy also accompanied him at all times. He waited in a room that could be accessed from the right side of the courtroom near the bailiff's desk. Kelley was held in an area that was just enough up and enough to the right of us that we could not see into it. I can say that the room had some sort of cell with a sliding metal door. We knew that because we could hear the sound of a metal door sliding open and closed when they brought him in and out of the courtroom each time. We assumed that Kelley was not handcuffed because the doorway of that room was not too many feet from where he was to sit.

We thought that the defendants were told not to look at anyone as they came and went. Although I do not know this for sure, I believe it is the case. Kelley always glanced around somewhat before sitting down. I surmised that he wanted to know who from his family might be there. He, too, wore slacks, a shirt but no tie.

If Kelley caught my eye I just looked straight at him. He may or may not have even known who I was at first. However, our family attended most of the hearings in which he appeared, so he must have known eventually. I think I was still looking for something in his glance, shame or regret. I never saw either, ever!

All along we assumed Ms. Wilson would stand trial with the two men since every time a new date was set she was included. It did not turn out as we thought. Remember, for her to be guilty of accessory after the fact Kelley would have to be found guilty of the crime. I really had a hard time understanding this when we where told that part of her charges included destroying evidence. Isn't that still wrong whether Kelley was found guilty or not? Her trial was "continued" until late January of 2009. She was never in attendance during the trial for Kelley and Nelson.

There were often valid reasons for those watching the proceedings to get up and leave the courtroom. However, it can be distracting for all involved. Judge Fasel encouraged us all early on to wait for one of the breaks to come and go, and if arriving late, to wait until a break to enter the courtroom. To my knowledge no one was turned away if delayed, at least not from our group.

I feel compelled to mention the chairs in the courtroom. Made of very thin plywood they were rigid and uncomfortable. In the area where we all sat, I believe there were six seats across and at least twelve or more rows back, but I am just guessing. I never officially counted. The same was true for the opposite side of the room. The middle section held even more seats across. Along the back of the room was another row of more seats that took up its whole length. As I mentioned, it was a very large room with capacity for numerous people.

No one was able sit in one position for too long because the seats were so hard. If you tried to adjust your position, the chair squeaked. It was almost humorous when there was a lull in conversation or testimony, many chairs squeaked at once! I, myself crossed one leg over the other and then frequently switched to the other leg to find a comfortable spot. I never did!

After everyone was seated, the bailiff got the jurors. They were the final group to enter the courtroom, having waited outside the door just like the rest of us. Yet another reason we had to be careful what we said and where we said it. I remember being so concerned about behaving correctly that I was almost afraid to make eye contact with them. If I did cross paths with a juror, I just smiled or said "good morning" but nothing else.

Several times a day the jurors, made up of eight women and six men including the two alternate's, filed past us. Some looked at us as they walked by and some did not. A few of the jurors carried notebooks and pens and some just had backpacks or a purse. We were not told which two were the alternates since all the jurors sat together. Thinking back, I am sure there must have been a designated spot for the pair but I do not know and should have asked but never did.

Judge Fasel was always the last person to enter the courtroom. There was never a call to "all rise" when he came in. The bailiff spoke up, telling us to remain in our seats and then said something like, "This court is in now called to order, the honorable Judge Fasel presiding."

Finally it was time for the opening statements. Brahim spoke of the defendants "total disregard for human life." Kelley's attorney claimed that Kelley acted in self-defense and feared the bouncers would hurt him and Nelson's attorney repeated over and over that his client had nothing to do with the stabbing.

The prosecution stated its case first. Due to the delay in jury selection some witnesses for the prosecution were ready to testify but had to wait. Hank, Herb and Steve waited two or more days to testify. Witnesses were not allowed in the courtroom to watch the proceedings until excused by the judge after their testimony was given.

At the beginning of each day, Brahim came over to where Riley and I sat, crouched down to the level of our seats, asked us how we were, and let us know what was to happen that day and who would be testifying. If I haven't said it enough he is the most caring man and how we were holding up was a priority to him. He ALWAYS warned us ahead of time when disturbing pictures or video were to be shown. He offered us the option of giving him a signal and being allowed to leave the courtroom. We never did take him up on that offer as hard as it often was to stay sometimes.

As it happened the trial actually started just as Colleen was ending her first semester at college. Her professors were reviewing material and she was preparing for finals. She missed as much class as she possibly could, often taking a final then racing to the courtroom. The poor baby had the added stress of wanting to be in court but needing to focus on finals. I felt so bad for her. She got through it and actually ended up doing very well.

Sean works as a bartender and moved his shifts around to be able to attend everyday. Riley is self employed so he tried to cram all he could onto Friday's when court was not in session and then worked the weekends. I had asked for the time off and given it back so many times that I finally just had a sit down conversation with my employers. It was agreed that when the trial was officially going to start I would just take the time off. I called daily to update them with how things were going and how long I might have to be gone. I was so thankful for their understanding and that I did not have to worry about my job on top of everything else.

I should mention that at the front of the courtroom stood a large poster on a stand that was referred to often in the coming days. On it were pictures of Brandon, Steve, Herb and some of the bouncers, the group of eight friends including Kelley and Nelson and their girlfriends as well as a picture of Ms. Wilson. Included as well were pictures of both the burgundy Corolla and white Saturn and an aerial view of the Tavern and the parking lot. In the coming days the parking lot became a very large topic of conversation.

The poster was big but the pictures on it were not. I may not be remembering all that was on the poster simply because it was a bit too far away from us. The poster was really meant to be in close proximity to the witness stand making it easy to access during testimony. The aerial view of the parking lot was a good size and we could see that very well from where we sat.

The Tavern is located in a business center or what I call a strip mall. The center is shaped like a rectangle. If you stood outside the Tavern, facing the parking lot, you saw several businesses. To the right, a car repair business, to the left a Dairy Queen and doughnut shop. Straight-ahead, across the three tiered parking area, a deli\market and karate business just to name a few.

Quite a bit of time was spent talking about the parking lot during the trial. The discussions included where the defendants were at any given moment, where the bouncers were, how the access roads on the sides and behind the center were used, who drove in which car, and which way the cars faced while parked.

In the coming days numerous people sat on the witness stand. As you will read in my daily emails, many testified on behalf of our son. However, some witnesses for the defense changed their stories and told untruths and out and out lies about what happened. Imagine having to sit day after day listening to the defense try and malign your son and his coworkers, all the while trying to remain emotionless.

During those times I sat there and dug my fingernails into the palm of my hand to try and stay composed. I saw Riley's jaw tighten as he fought to remain in control.

Those days were the hardest. Our son was not there to defend himself, could not be there, he was dead! He was not the one on trial yet we sat there as witnesses for the defense tried to paint him and his character in a bad light.

The level of exhaustion I felt was something I had never experienced before. I wanted to stand up so many times, right there in the court room and scream! Nelson never looked at us as I mentioned but when Kelley's eye caught mine by chance or by his intention, I still saw no glimmer of remorse, sadness or sorrow for what he had done. This was a man who had committed acts of violence before and it was so very hard to have to see him, to see the both of them every day.

I have added the first of my daily emails here. Since they were all written at the end of each day my memory was much clearer and I am so glad I wrote them. They have really helped me keep the events straight in my head. I have also added more comments after each email where appropriate. I removed all the email addresses for the privacy of the recipients and left the spelling and grammar as originally written so please excuse any grammatical errors, I was usually a bit tired by the time I sat down to write.

Sent: Wednesday, December 03, 2008 5:05 PM
Subject: Trial update

Well, it was hurry up and wait day today. Thank you to all that were there today lending support. It means so much. Most of us ended up staying and had meetings with the DA and it was helpful to him. Just heard from DA Brahim and jury selection is done after 2 full days so we are on for tomorrow. Yesterday a juror had a seizure (delayed things by about 3 hours) and another juror broke down and said she was a friend of Brandon's and had to be excused. But as of 5pm today all are chosen.

Turns out we were misinformed about the parking and the buildings on either side of the courthouse are the ones to park in. They validated ours from the other parking lot and we were not charged but I don't know if that will work every day.

Anyone who can attend tomorrow should meet on the second floor by the DA offices as we did today because they want to have us all come in together before the jury is seated. Looks better I guess and they will show you where to validate parking as well as more instruction and where we are to sit.

Again thanks to all who were there today, we love you all, Erin

Sent: Thursday, December 04, 2008 5:48 PM
Subject: trial update

Thank you to all of you who have been able to attend the last two days. It means so much to us to have your support. There were about 30 of us I think today. Kelley had who we think may have had family there and a couple of friends and we saw no one for Nelson but we cannot be sure. There were 4 Sheriffs in the room at all times.

Things have finally started and we are learning that it is a S L O W W W W process. Brahim gave opening statements, as did the 2 defense attorneys. The first deputy to the scene that night was called to testify as well as Kelley's (former it seems) girlfriend. She was interesting and that is all I will say for now. Not really too willing. Hard to follow and the things she said to the Grand Jury are not the things she said today in some statements. She is excused for today but could be called back. Next was Hank, the head bouncer at the Tavern, a very nice man. At 4:30 they stopped things til Monday and Hank will come back. So far and the case is FAR from getting really going but you can tell Brahim is building a case with the questions he is asking. The bouncers were just doing their jobs dealing with 2 men who wanted to fight so far. There are disturbing statements and pictures already and that is very hard.

Ok I am keeping it short. We are worn out. Again thank you to all, Erin

As I mentioned before there was no court for us on Fridays. That day is reserved for other types of one-day cases. That is why you see a jump in dates from December 5th to December 8th.

Subject: Trial update December 8th 9:24 PM
Hello all,

First of all thank you to all of those who have attended the trial with us. To have others there with us has been so comforting and I know it is an effort especially for those juggling work to be there. We will NEVER forget your caring.

Today was a difficult day. The Coroner spoke and there were autopsy pictures. The DA warned us ahead (another reason I admire him) and I was relieved that Colleen had class this morning and missed it but don't tell her that. She does not know we saw pictures and arrived as if by magic at the morning break after it all.

The wound was classified as a stab rather than a slash (which we surmised meant more intent) and affected Brandon's trachea as well as an artery that provides blood to the thyroid and to the heart. The other hard thing to hear was testimony from his good friend and fellow bouncer Steve who held the wound as best he could and friend and fellow bouncer who is an active Navy corpsman, Bryan who did his best to help as well. To know our son was in pain and feared he would die was very emotional for us when I had convinced myself he was in shock immediately and did not feel pain.

Tomorrow, friend and bouncer Herb will testify after being there waiting for 3 days and unable to be in the courtroom. Also the chief investigator Joe will testify. He has been at Brahim's side throughout the trial and is also a wonderful man who was instrumental in getting Nelson arrested.

Brahim feels things are going well and he is "getting out" all that he wants to. As of today he thinks closing statements will be the afternoon of Monday or Tuesday some time but it is a slow process so I will know more by the end of the week. Closing statements sort of tie everything in a neat package so is an important day. There is also a chance that Kelley will testify on his own behalf. It is rare for a defendant to testify at their own trial but if he is claiming self defense he must testify. To have a defendant testify on his own behalf does not typically work out in favor of the defendant. If he does his past police record would be admissible which would be good for us. If he does not his past cannot be brought up until sentencing. After closing statements we will need to be close by while the jury deliberates. You must be on a 20 minute call because once a verdict is decided upon it is given with or with out the family there.

Sitting in the courtroom is very surreal and as I sat there today I could not help but think "what the hell am I doing here".

Ok that is most of it for today. Love you all, Erin

Subject: Trial update Dec 9. 2008 9:20 PM

Hello,

Another long day of testimony. Today bouncer and good friend Herb testified. He did a great job and we were able to hear his side of things and how he got the knife away and how he was injured. He also slashed the tires of the car he believed was involved in the crime so the car could not get away. Herb may face another surgery on his hand. They cannot figure out why he cannot move his index finger. DNA showed, and it was confusing but I think I got it. Herb's, Brandon's and Kelley's DNA were on the inside of the slashed tires. Brandon, Herb and Steve (the three injured that night) and Kelley's DNA on the knife. Kelley's and Brandon's under the seat of the car Kelley was in, the Burgundy Corolla.

Next a wonderful man Joe, the lead investigator testified. He is the nicest man and he and his team has worked so hard on this case.

There are SO many facets to all this, it makes your head reel. I am doing my best to be accurate. Again I believe we now know that Nelson and Kelley's girlfriend, at the time, are cousins. Ms. Wilson who is the one who destroyed evidence is their Aunt and it is her home in Hesperia that Kelley ultimately was driven to by Ms. Wilson that morning. Her son was one of the 8 people who all were together that night. The 8 involved were staying at the other couples house in Laguna Beach for the holiday weekend. THAT is how they ended up at the Tavern. The couples had been to the Tavern before.

We are talking of about 5 hours of testimony so it is hard to recount it all. The knife measured about 8 inches with a 4-inch blade that curved at the end. Nelson who is accused of murder for starting the whole verbal part, which led to Brandon's death, was wearing a "grill" that night. That was talked about a lot. A grill is teeth jewelry and they are not cheap but it positively identified him as one who had caused trouble in the bar.

The prosecution rested and 3 witnesses for the defense took the stand. WOW! I have told you how wonderful Brahim is but he transformed into a different person and tore their stories up. First was Nelson's (former) girlfriend. Neither Kelley's nor Nelson's girlfriends at the time had seen the two of them for one year. She seemed not to be a real credible witness. Next was another female friend that was there with them. She was another in the group who had trouble remembering what she told the sheriffs in interviews. Next was Mr. Scott, who was there with them as well and had known Kelley and Nelson for many years but, and this is where it is confusing, has prior felonies, for what they don't say, but is known "for not being truthful". So why does the defense put on a witness who is not known for telling the truth? He was mad he had to wait to talk to the cops after the incident so made up stuff about what went on then changed his story.

So, tomorrow Kelley will take the stand. He can still change his mind but he is scheduled and it may take the whole day. Everyone is waiting to hear his side of things. It is risky as I said before for him to testify, but if he is claiming self-defense he must. Brahim made a point all day to ask everyone if Kelley ever mentioned that he had been in an altercation that night and had to defend himself and they all said no.

Ok I am tired, more later. Love to all, Erin

I failed to mention in my nightly emails what a great job Steve and Herb did testifying. I know it was so hard for both of them. The defense tried several time to rattle Steve, shooting questions at him, trying to confuse him and trip him up. I believe Brahim objected to the line of questioning several times while he testified. Steve kept his cool; stayed calm and simply told the truth.

Subject: Trial update Dec 10th, 2008 9:29PM
As I write this, Riley and I, Sean and Colleen are asleep on our feet.

Today the "killer" as Brahim calls him; Kelley took the stand in his own defense. His story is a bit different from the bouncers. He states that he had the knife on him (changing his original story to the police that he knew nothing about a knife) that night as well as the other night that he and his friends were at the Tavern. For protection he says and he used it for work. It is NOT a work knife by the look and has a curved blade about 4 inches and the handle is 4 inches. Brahim asked him if he was planning on doing a roofing job after being at the Tavern New Years Eve to which he replied no. Even though the bouncers at the door pat the men down before they enter the bar he states it was not found either time he had been at the Tavern. Hmmm... He states that he was in a car with Mr. Scott and wanted to "get outa there" but when Mr. Scott realized that his girlfriend was still there turned his car around and went back and told Kelley to stay in the car which he did not. He states that a person he identified as Brandon and Steve (slashed in jaw Steve) were coming at him and he, Kelley felt threatened and brought out his knife and he did slash around but says did not know he cut anyone. It was proved by the coroner that Brandon's wound was not a slash but a stab, remember. Someone who he cannot identify got the knife away from him and he does not know where the knife went. All he knows is that there was a "pile" of people on him and then all of the sudden there weren't (that must have been when everyone realized that Brandon was injured and went to his aid). He got in a car (the burgundy Corolla) and left with his girlfriend and went back to Laguna Beach and then shortly after was driven by Ms. Wilson to her house in Hesperia. I am not sure if I told you that Kelley's girlfriend states she stepped in something wet (lost her shoes at some point I guess) but cannot say what it was and says she never looked. Even though the pair drove back to Laguna Beach and onto Hesperia she contends that she never looked at her feet. Part of what Ms. Wilson is accused of is removing the plastic cover that is often on the pedals of new cars (they had only had their new Corolla for a week or so) The pedal had blood on it from Kelley's girlfriend's feet. I believe and so did the prosecution that what she stepped in was

Brandon's blood as they fled the scene. Ms. Wilson is not in the courtroom during this trial since she was not involved until after the fact. Kelley claims he did not find out that anyone died or was injured until later. He was scared and lied to the police when interviewed. Brahim is trying to show that he was protecting Nelson who caused a lot of trouble fighting at the Tavern but Kelley denies that. Did I say they were and are best friends since childhood? Brahim brought up Kelley's prior convictions and gang affiliations and Kelley claims he moved to Big Bear to get away from all that. I spoke to bouncer Steve and he says that is not how it happened. Kelley claims that Brandon and Steve "came at him" and he feared for his life. What he actually said when initially interviewed was that the bouncers "headed him off". There was also not a "pile of people" on him it was just Steve.

Today when Kelley admitted the knife was his it was a relief for us. He had denied anything to do with a knife initially. He says he did not go back to a car and get it as everyone else is saying and none of the people with him including his then girlfriend who he lived with and had a child with knew he had a knife that night.

In the middle of things today the defense attorney for Nelson called for a mis-trial when Brahim showed Kelley some pictures of Kelley and Nelson on the wall in Wilson's house. The judge looked angry and called for a side bar (they do that a lot during the day) and denied the motion. It was confusing and I am not really sure what that was all about.

After the jury was dismissed for the day the Judge and all attorney's met and we got to watch as the defense asked for permission to call 2 witnesses from an incident at Hennessey's for which Brandon was fired. They will fly in from another state. Montana I believe. If I didn't ever say Brandon started bouncing at the Tavern and moved later to Hennessey's. He said he was bored at the Tavern but I do not know for sure. Maybe Hennessey's paid more. He was head bouncer at Hennessey's at the time he was let go and was instrumental in getting the bouncers the earpieces by which they communicated. I remember days and days of Ebay deliveries of headpieces that he purchased and I believe he was reimbursed for. Anyway I do not know the whole story but one night a family who was there to celebrate the marriage of their son came into Hennessey's. When the bartender accidentally gave them the wrong credit card back they got angry. It would have been an easy fix but the family started causing trouble. From what I was told Bran did not come in til later but the family threatened to sue Hennessey's claiming their son was injured that night and to my knowledge the matter was settled but corporate wanted to make an example and fired Brandon. Josh and Herb and most of the other bouncers quit on the spot in protest. Brandon went back to the Tavern and was rehired. It was 2 weeks before Christmas and he needed to pay rent! Others followed him to the Tavern to work. From what I was told the family asked who the manager was and they were told it was Brandon, which is not true. He was head bouncer not manager. The family spoke to the manager and called him Brandon. I know it is confusing but it sounds like mistaken identity. The judge after much debate is allowing the witnesses even though Brahim argued that the defense is trying to paint Brandon in a bad light. The defense says that while Brandon may be a wonderful person out side the bar that he was aggressive at work. It will be another difficult day tomorrow however Brahim has witnesses to dispute the family's story about Brandon's involvement in the altercation. We will have to sit there while they deface our son who cannot defend himself but we were warned this was likely.

Please pardon my wordy email. It is hard to say all that goes on but this is the jist of it. Our minds are numb, our bodies sore from the very hard seats and the stress is incredible. As of this moment and it changes daily, closing statements could be Tuesday. Then we must wait for deliberation.

If I was worried about any trouble from the defendant's friends it is so far so good. There is PLENTY of Sheriff presence in our courtroom and our judge is very strict and people are asked to leave if misbehaving. We all sit with hands folded and get no looks of discontent from the judge. Our jury is attentive and there are 8 women and 6 men including the 2 alternates who are there the whole time so we do not know which ones they are.

Thank you to all who have asked for this email. At least 60 at last count. Take care, Erin

It was refreshing to hear that after initially denying he had a knife at all, Kelley admitted the knife was his and that he used it for work and protection. He said he had had it in his pocket both times the group visited the Tavern and the bouncers never felt it in his pocket. The bouncers are taught to check for weapons and know the difference between a cell phone and a knife. Brahim felt that Kelley had not been truthful when he stated that he had the knife on him when first entering the bar that night.

115

It was hard to have to look directly at Kelley while he testified. He was not intimidating looking and I was not afraid to look at him but imagine staring straight at the man who stabbed your son in the neck, killing him and remaining calm as you sat twenty feet away.

In the following email I write about a father and son who falsely accused Brandon of manhandling their son. Brandon was the head bouncer at Hennessey's in Dana Point at the time. The alleged altercation resulted in his termination. Even though their names are public record and I need not seek their permission to name them, I have chosen not to. I feel nothing but anger at their actions and accusations. Mentioning their names did not warrant wasting the print. In fact the son could not even look at Riley and I as he walked past us after his testimony. Witness after witness will dispute their claims.

Sent: Dec 11, 2008 6:27 PM
To: Subject: Trial update December 11
I realized that the only way I know it is Thursday today is from my Sunday - Saturday pill organizer that I keep my vitamins etc in, pretty sad.

This morning was a difficult one. The defense got permission to bring 2 witnesses from Montana that I may have mentioned before who got in a scuffle with the bouncers at Hennessey's in December of 2006 resulting in Brandon being fired, a father and son. They identified Brandon as one who they allege mistreated and manhandled them. They made it sound like Brandon was a one man wrecking crew. Brandon was not involved in the altercation until after it was well under way and that was to help restrain a family member who was causing trouble. It was hard to sit there and have to listen to them, but the DA warned us. The whole afternoon we listened to testimony after testimony of the bouncer's side of it and that there may have been some mistaken identity on the part of the family. When talking to Brandon the father referred to him as the man who actually was the manager on duty that day. He was head bouncer not manager. Bouncers, co workers and good friends including Josh, Jesse, Vince (who has 3 purple hearts and 2 Navy crosses) and Jerod testified about the family's aggressions towards the bouncers and about Brandon as a person, his calm nature and that he tried to defuse issues in the bar with words rather than actions, his loyalty and leadership. A manager at Hennessey's testified as well stating that Brandon was made head bouncer because of these traits.

The deputy Sheriff who arrested Kelley in Hesperia also testified and while he did not investigate the crime because he was just sent to pick him up said they do write in their report word for word what is said by anyone and in essence Kelley said he had been in the OC and involved in a fight and "messed up." Never telling the officer he feared for his life or that he acted in self-defense. Brahim brings up that fact *a lot* that Kelley never ever told anyone he feared for his life until his testimony in court. He also lied about having a knife when questioned initially. As I said he claims he had the knife on him the whole time even though he is seen getting something from the trunk of the car and hiding it behind his back. No one actually saw what sort of weapon only saw him hide something.

At the end of today the jury is dismissed and we stayed to listen in on a motion from Kelley's lawyer to deny Brahim bringing in a man that Kelley assaulted in the past. Long story short, each side regarding the questions that will be asked makes agreements. The judge denied the motion to deny the witness so that man will testify on Monday as well as possibly more character witnesses for Brandon. The plan is that closing statements will be Tuesday morning and then we go to the cafeteria and wait for the jury to deliberate. The closing statement is where Brahim brings the whole thing together including Nelson's involvement. The lawyer for Nelson has over and over again stressed that Nelson did not kill Brandon or injure Steve or Herb, which is true. The judge must inform the jury about the law regarding Nelson's instigation of the fighting which lead to the death of our son and injury to his wonderful friends. It is up to the jury. Brahim says that closing statement day is a great day to be there to understand all so anyone who can be there is welcome.

My next update will be on Monday as there is no court for us tomorrow. They reserve that day for civil cases.

Please keep us in your prayers. Love to all, Erin

Sent: Mon, 15 Dec 2008 5:21 pm
Subject: Trial update Dec 15

Hello my friends. Well the prosecution rested and the defense rested but not without a few more little "guests" that Brahim arranged for. First was a man from Oregon who Kelley assaulted with a beer bottle in 1998 over the color of the guys shoes (we are confused too, but they were supposed to be gang colors I think), second was a letter put into evidence and agreed to by all 3 attorney's stating that Kelley had in 2000 assaulted a man (hit him with a champagne bottle) after taking his cell phone and when the man got out of his car and went to a pay phone to call 911 he hit him with the bottle. Also in the letter it was stated that the man who they brought from Montana (who said Brandon "chokeholded" his son and kicked him in the head) said in his statement at the time of the incident that he wasn't sure if his son was even kicked in the head or by whom. He also testified in this trial that the bartender had a bat behind the bar and in this letter his statement at the time never mentioned a bat. It is our understanding from testimony that Brandon never "chokeholded" anyone during the altercation. Also if there was any confusion in my previous email, Kelley's DNA was on the knife. Previously I thought I heard that only the 3 victims DNA was on the knife. Herb's was inside the slashed tire as well and Brandon's and Kelley's under the seat in the car.

Next was a very nice man, a patron of Hennessey's who frequented the bar with 3 friends (all doctors) at least twice a week. He testified that he never saw Brandon act in a violent manner and was always professional and friendly. In fact one night he and his friends were there and at a table next to them, 2 guys started getting into it and Brandon came over to defuse it. They started up again and when Brandon intervened again one of them spit at my kid! They were removed from the bar but the patron stated Brandon acted professionally at all times.

Next the courtroom locked down for Jury instructions. Usually this is done just prior to deliberations but there was time this day so the judge decided to do the instructions today. This means if you want to stay you may but you may not leave during this time. No one from the defense supporters stayed. This is a long process but interesting. The jury is instructed as to how to make their conclusions and what the law is.

Brahim told us later that he is optimistic (but he always says that) but that he did his very best and got all the information out that he wanted to and now it is up to the jury. We truly love this man! We know he did everything he could and he knows how we feel about him.

Closing statements are at 9am tomorrow and will wrap everything up in a nice package we are told. Any who can attend are welcome and you know to dress appropriately etc. Brahim speaks first then both defense attorneys and then Brahim gets a chance to speak again. After that it is the cafeteria for us, too wait. You may not be any farther away than 20 min or less. If the verdict comes in they read it whether you are there or not. Sentencing is 4-6 weeks after the verdict.

So many of you have taken this journey with us and for that I thank you. We have so appreciated the support and expect a big crowd tomorrow. The trial has been emotionally, physically and mentally draining and we have so many people to thank for their work on the proceedings, especially, Brahim and his team from the District Attorney's office. Joe the lead investigator, who was there with Kelley at his arrest on January 1, 2007 and has been there with us throughout, Dina, another investigator, who organized the witnesses, as well as Melissa, our liaison from the Victim's Assistance Office. All have worked tirelessly for Brandon. Brahim has had Brandon's picture in his office since we met about 2 days after his death and Brahim says he looks at it everyday to remember who he works for.

Keep praying for us and that the jury will be swift. Love, Erin

Brahim actually considered putting me on the witness stand when gathering character witnesses. He must have noticed the stricken, wide-eyed look I got on my face at the suggestion. I inwardly panicked thinking, "What if they twist my words, what if I say the wrong thing!" I told him I would testify if he needed me to. I am not sure if it was my nervous reaction or what, but in the end, Brahim told us he had decided to call in regular patrons, who would have seen Brandon doing his job, instead.

Through it all, Joe Gaul was there every day at Brahim's side in the courtroom. He even spent time to go back to the Tavern during a lunch break. There had been a question about who could see what from where when the burgundy Corolla, with Kelley in it, came back around from the ally behind the deli/market towards the Tavern (when Mr. Scott realized that his girlfriend was still at the bar and went back to get her). I think the question was whether Kelley could possibly see Nelson in the parking lot from where Mr. Scott had stopped the car. I believe it was determined that he could.

Closing statements were the opportunity for both the prosecution and the defense to recap testimony and remind the jury of their objectives while deliberating.

Sent: Tuesday, December 16, 2008 8:06 PM
Subject: Trial update December 16 "Wait, it gets better"

Today was a VERY tense and the longest of all the days in the courtroom. I will explain my subject line in a minute. We had over 50+ supporters today and filled our section of the courtroom and then some, from family to friends to bouncers to co-workers. It was amazing and the jury notices that. The defense had more than usual but maybe 10-12 instead of the usual 4-5. Along with all of that were other attorney's listening to the closing statements as well as a definite police presence? Usually we have 4 today there were 5 all day.

First of all when the jurors sat down there was an obvious problem. A missing juror! We all had to wait while they tried to figure it out and by the end of the day we still did not know what happened to him. I sat there fearing that after all these days a mistrial would be called. We are hoping to find out but the judge said it is not to be spoken of. He was not a happy judge. It was pouring rain so we wondered if the juror was stuck somewhere. After a meeting "in chambers" one of the alternate jurors was sworn in. Hopefully nothing horrible happened to the other juror but he will have some splainin to do. It is not a good thing that he listened to testimony for almost 2 weeks and then is a no show. After a delay of almost an hour the closing statements started with DA Brahim. He stated again that among other things that Kelley and Nelson had a total disregard for human life and both had Brandon's blood soaking their hands.

Brahim went point-by-point explaining the law and how the jurors would use that in their deliberations. What the different degrees of murder are, what attempted murder is, assault with a deadly weapon etc. He built the story of what happened that night disputing Kelley's self defense claim in many ways but one that sticks in my mind. Kelley did not leave that night even when the bouncers offered to call a cab for them and their girlfriends said "let's just go" but Nelson and Kelley both took off their shirts to reveal white tank tops (Brahim called them their "fighting uniforms") showing they were ready for a fight. In fact Kelley pushed his then girlfriend away when she tried to get him to leave, remember? After leaving the bar Kelley and the girlfriend went back to Hesperia and went to sleep even knowing someone had died that night. Turns out the call his girlfriend claimed was made to the police was never made. We had to view the autopsy pictures again but were warned prior by Brahim. Brahim spoke of the "white rose of truth" coming out among the garbage that and I understood he was speaking of certain testimony of the defense.

As Brahim was building his story he would keep saying, "Wait, it gets better." His closing took all morning and after lunch it was Kelley's attorneys turn. She tried to negate alot of the testimony of Brandon's friends and co-workers as their attempt to help Brandon and getting revenge. She tried to say they all treated each other as family therefore would try and make Brandon look good. She also, in our eyes and the eyes of all, there committed character assassination of Brandon, bringing up AGAIN the incident at Hennessey's. But the jurors heard it again. She recounted all the boy's height and weight and is trying to say that Kelley was afraid for his life because of their size. She twisted testimony around and especially Steve (who was there today trying his best to stay in his chair). Between Steve and Riley wanting to jump out of his chair it was tense. The judge called a break after she spoke.

After the break Nelson's attorney still states over and over in his closing that his client is innocent of all crime. "He was a moron" who picked a fight but had no knowledge of a knife or that Kelley intended to do harm. Nelson's attorney stood behind Kelley and in essence said this is the man that killed Brandon, not my client. Just so you know according to Brahim the law states he does not have to know about the knife but Brahim thinks he did know about it. Nelson's attorney said his client was drunk and did start a fight but had no knowledge of a knife and in fact was nowhere near Kelley, a fact that Brahim will argue.

Then because of the way things work "the People" get the last word. Do not ask me where Brahim got the time to power point every thing both attorneys said since we only had a 20 min break after Nelson's attorney ended and Brahim was to start up again. He asked if everyone was ready to come back to earth from "La La land". He had up on a screen point by point and refuted (is that the word) everything that was said. He defended Steve's testimony and called Kelley's attorney on twisting it. We were very upset after the closings statements of the 2 defense attorneys with all the twisting of the truth and then there is Brahim. He would make a point and then over and over saying, "wait, it gets better".

The last thing the jurors saw was a smiling picture of Brandon up on his screen. About broke our hearts to see his face and that beautiful smile. Now it is up to them to understand the law and decide the fate of these 2 men. There seems to be no doubt that Kelley killed Brandon but in what degree and was it self defense as stated by the defense. The defense is very thin but it is in the jury's hands. Brahim told us again tonight that he did his very best and got to say all he wanted to say. He feels the jurors are reasonable.

Tomorrow we will be there at 9 when the jurors come in to show a presence. Then we wait. You cannot be more than 20 minutes away. The verdict is read when it comes in. We have come this far and must see this to the end as hard as that is. We hope the decision will be swift but the jurors may want to review testimony so no one can say. Brahim hopes by the end of the week. My next email will be with the verdict. If I haven't said it enough thank you all and for those who have been with us every day, some days, one hour or by email. thank you, thank you, Erin

I wanted to include Brahim's speech, taken word for word, from the court transcripts of the closing statements regarding the "white rose of truth." For me it was a very profound part of his closing statements and the inspiration for the title of my book. Brahim said:

"You know, there is absolutely, categorically, nothing pleasant or beautiful about a murder trial. It is just—it is full of unpleasantness. You get to hear about the last moment of a young man. It is full of ugliness. It is just full of ugliness. But the minute you come across these doors and 12 decent, law-abiding, honest, full of common sense jurors decide to do their civic duty and do their job, there is always something beautiful, always something beautiful about a trial in a murder case. I always think about it. I think about this never-ending field of trash. Just think about this. You can imagine a field full of trash. It is garbage, full of garbage. Then, right in the middle of it, just right in the middle as the trial progresses, you get closer. It is just a white rose starts coming out. A white rose starts coming out, out, out. And it is the truth. It is the truth. There is absolutely nothing more beautiful than the truth. It can break your heart. It can make you feel agony and hurt and sadness. But it is beautiful. It is absolutely beautiful. The truth comes out."

All of us listening to his speech felt that the "garbage" he referred to was a metaphor for what the defense was trying to make everyone accept as the truth. They wanted us to believe that Kelley acted in self-defense.

After lunch break Kelley's attorney spoke as I stated in my email. She stated that the bouncers treat each other as family and would say things to make Brandon look good.

We were all pretty depressed after listening to Kelley's attorney trying to smear our son's reputation. I remember feeling so very anxious. I was not sure what was going to happen next. Were the last words the jury heard destined to be so very negative?

I glanced over at Brahim several times while Kelley's attorney was speaking and he was always writing. I assumed he was taking notes on what was being said, but have never asked him. He just continued to write, only looking up occasionally. We did not have an opportunity to speak to Brahim during the break as we often did and now I know why he disappeared. He had been preparing for his rebuttal. I still do not know how Brahim, in twenty minutes, organized an argument to every point made by the defense.

I recall that my heart swelled with renewed hope and it was like the cavalry had arrived and charged in on white horses! Everyone on our side of the room sat up a bit straighter in their seats as he spoke. I wish I could have cheered.

I want to mention the "rule of three" Brahim spoke about that day and also the "rule of one."

Brahim referred to the rule of three during his closing statements. He was referring to lies Kelley told and then tried to cover up. Brahim said that lying is not easy. In fact it is one of the hardest things to do.

For example, Kelley testified that, on both occasions that he visited the Tavern he had the knife in his pocket the whole time. Brahim thought that was "laughable." Kelley knew that he could not get into the bar with his knife and that is how it ended up back in the white car, along with an Angel's baseball cap that Nelson knew he could not wear in the bar due to the no hat rule.

Rule number 1, you have to remember the truth because you want to stay away from it. Number 2, you are thinking of your prior lies because you don't want your prior lies to contradict or be contradicted. Number 3, you are thinking about your current lie because you don't want your current lie to contradict prior lies or come close to the truth. That is the rule of three.

Kelley was caught in another lie. He claimed that he acted in self-defense, that he brought out the knife and swung it around. But, nobody saw the stabbing, by design, Brahim explained. Steve testified that he never saw what hit him. That was Kelley's intention, according to Brahim.

Brahim's last question to Kelley on the witness stand was "As far as you know, let me ask you this. Did you show the knife to anybody that night, anybody?" Kelley's answer was "no, no." Brahim then asked, "Never showed the knife, said "hey, get back I have a knife?" Kelley's answered that he never showed the knife to anybody. Even though he claimed to have brought the knife out and swung it around. Kelley seemed to go right for the necks of both Brandon and Steve. Not the stomach, or arm or leg, but the neck. Brahim was sure that if Kelley could take that last "no" answer back, he would.

Kelley left a crime scene and lied to the police on several occasions, changing his story. There was no credible evidence that he was in fear of death or great bodily injury that night at the Tavern.

Brahim also referred to the rule of one. He spoke to the jury, "Are they really thinking that 12 people are going to buy the self-defense or that Nelson had nothing to do with it? They, (meaning the defense) don't want 12, they want 1. Because if one juror takes his or her focus away from the law and the facts, if one juror takes his or her focus away from the evidence and from your duty you can't get a conviction. That's all it takes." That is the rule of one. I sat there and thought "wow" it could not have been said better than that.

As I wrote in my email, at the end of Brahim's final statement he showed a huge picture of Brandon up on the big screen. It was an enlargement of the picture we had given to Brahim the first time we met him. It was also the picture we chose for Brandon's marker at the gravesite. At the bottom of the picture words were added, Born: May 4, 1985, Murdered: January 1, 2007. I was not prepared for such a large picture to be displayed, and for the first time during the whole trial process, I cried openly. We had all been stoic through out the trial. I thought to myself," what the hell", at that moment, as my tears flowed.

I had held it together for two weeks and if the jury saw me cry, the judge or the defendant's family, I didn't care at that point. That was my son up there on that screen, my baby boy! Never would I get another one of his big bear hugs, never see him smile that stunning smile or laugh that magnificent laugh ever again. So, yes, I cried and so did Riley and half the courtroom.

I assumed the picture was shown to make a lasting impression on everyone in the room and also to remind the jury just who the last two weeks had been about. We have seen that picture many times and it is one of my favorite photos of him but to see it larger than life up on the screen was very hard.

The Deliberations

Judge Fasel adjourned court for the day. Before he did, the second alternate juror was excused with the understanding that he might be asked to come back if needed, in a prearranged, agreed upon, amount of time. I believe the juror agreed that he could return within forty-five minutes of receiving a phone call from the court. To my knowledge he had to be available until deliberations were complete.

The following day, December 17, 2008 deliberations began. We were advised that a show of support was often helpful and demonstrated our resolve to see justice served. The four of us, joined by a few others drove to the courthouse, and were at the doorway of the courtroom by 9 a.m. We were let in and waited until the jurors filed passed us, led by the bailiff.

We just watched them as they walked by. The jury deliberated in a room accessible by a door located at the very front of our courtroom. They all walked past us, in a single line, past the jury box where they had listened to testimony for the last two weeks, past the witness stand and through the doorway just ahead. The door closed and that was that. They all saw us sitting there in our usual spots and that was what was important.

Our group then went to the cafeteria to wait. As the morning wore on, more people arrived to sit with us. It was a cold, rainy, miserable day outside and we felt bad for anyone who drove over in such horrible weather. However, we were ever so grateful for the company.

As I have mentioned, there were often more than a few sheriff's deputies in our courtroom. Two bailiffs were there every day. One of them told us that the rule of thumb was usually one day of deliberations per each week of the trial. Taking that into account, we assumed we would be there for a couple of days at least.

We did have, during the course of the trial, the pleasure to meet a family that waited in the cafeteria for a verdict in a trial that involved the murder of a family member. It was nice to meet another family who could relate to what we had just gone through the past two weeks. I believe theirs was a "cold case" that the first time around, ended in a hung jury and was being re-tried. They had been waiting nine days already for a verdict! Nine days of sitting in the cafeteria waiting for news. I do not believe, that in the end, they got the verdict they were hoping for, after all that time...

We had never even considered how long deliberations might take. We hadn't thought about it. All of us just wanted to get through each day of the trial. When we met that family and found out that we could conceivably be there for days and days waiting for a verdict, it was a scary and unnerving feeling.

The jury had the option to ask for any transcripts, photos or video from the proceedings to help them during the process. If they needed to refresh their memories or revisit any testimony to help them with their decision, it would be provided.

As we sat in the cafeteria, right on schedule the jurors came in for their morning break. Conversation became very quiet at our table and everyone held off talking about anything to do with the trial. Any juror that wished to take their break in the cafeteria may do so. We saw them scattered throughout the room.

It was freezing in the cafeteria that day so around 11:30 a.m. while Colleen was talking on her cell phone to Molly; I chimed in and asked if Molly might bring me a blanket when she came. I know part of my problem was nerves. I was very cold and it was pouring rain outside so Molly agreed to bring me something to wrap around my shoulders.

Colleen no sooner got off the phone when Brahim called my cell phone to say that a verdict had been reached and that it would be read at 1:30 pm after the jurors lunch break.

"Oh my God!" they had decided already! We were all in shock! How could there be a verdict so quickly? Was this a good thing or a bad thing? Didn't they need more time? Did a quick verdict mean that the two defendants had been found guilty so fast or not guilty so fast? So many questions went through all of our heads. My heart was pounding!

I had mentioned earlier how texting would become important. This was where it became very important. Within minutes, we had frantically contacted as many people as we could to let them know the news. Thank goodness for the group text option!

Guy had come to sit with us that morning. Since we were unsure how long we might be waiting he decided to go to a local mall to do some Christmas shopping. He asked that we call him and he would come right back, which he did. My sister Sheila offered her support that morning as well. We were so sure nothing was going to happen that day, I told her she might as well go onto work. Sheila, in the rain, came all the way back to be with us. She, along with over forty friends and family dropped everything and in less than ninety minutes arrived at the courthouse to hear the verdict.

During this frantic time of phone calls and texts, the jurors came into the cafeteria for their lunch break. They knew the verdict but there was no way to tell by their faces. They all seemed happy enough but that could mean anything. They could have been happy it was lunchtime, happy for us, for the defendants or happy deliberations were over. We tried not to look at them but it was hard not to search their faces for some clue. We got none. It was the longest hour of my life!

The Verdict

Date: Dec 17, 2008 8:02 PM

Hello all, Wow, what a day. We were told by one of the bailiffs that the rule of thumb was 1 day of deliberation per week of testimony so we were prepared for the long haul. We and a few friends appeared in the court room today to show a presence as the jurors walked by through the courtroom to the deliberation room and then set up for a long wait in the cafeteria at 9:30 ish. The jurors took a break at 10:30 (we saw them enter the cafeteria) and I got a call at noon from Brahim saying the verdict was going to be read at 1:30. 3 hours of deliberation only!!!! There was a flurry of phone calls and mass text messaging and at least 40 people drove in as support. It was pouring rail again and those who came dropped everything to be there with us and at such short notice! It was amazing! It seemed to take forever for the judge to read the verdict to himself before he handed it to the court secretary to read out loud. It has to have been at least five minutes and was like an eternity! Kelley stared right at me as he was lead in. It was an uncomfortable moment but I stared right back at him. I saw such evil in his eyes. It is hard to explain. Nelson never looked at any of us. Kelley had his head in his hands as the verdicts were read:

KELLEY, GUILTY of Murder in the first degree of Brandon and KELLEY, GUILTY of Attempted murder of Steve. KELLEY, GUILTY of assault with a deadly weapon GUILTY as charged on all counts!!!!

NELSON, GUILTY of Murder in the first degree of Brandon and NELSON, GUILTY of Attempted murder of Steve. NELSON. GUILTY as charged on all counts even though he did not do the stabbing he was found just as guilty as Kelley.

Nelson found guilty for instigating the events that lead to Brandon's death. Both convicted unanimously!!!!!!

We were told to not react if the verdict was good or bad but Riley and I cried.

The verdict will not bring our son back, will not bring "closure" accept for the knowledge that these two men will not hurt anybody else and that justice was served for our son. We still feel that his death is so surreal and miss him so but are so relieved to be done with this difficult part and are so thankful to all of you for sharing it with us.

The whole homicide team that worked on our case was in the courtroom. We got the thank each of the 8 of them. The nice man from the Register News Paper was there and spoke to us, so watch the paper. There was no one present for either of the defendants. I suppose they too thought deliberations would take longer, I do not know.

We are tired beyond words but so very thankful and happy. Sentencing will be in February 20, 2009 and we are told we can wear anything we want to commemorate Brandon on that day.

Thank you again to all, and to all a good night!!! Erin

Kelley sat with his head in his hands as the court secretary announced the verdicts. Nelson, as usual had no reaction. Every time a verdict was read Brahim turned around and looked at Riley and I, as if to confirm that justice had been served. Five times our eyes met his in silent triumph. After court was adjourned we were able to hug Brahim, Joe and several others who had worked so hard over the last two years. As we all left the courtroom, Riley and I stopped to talk to reporter Larry Welborn from "The Orange County Register", who had covered Brandon's murder since the day it happened. He was a frequent visitor in the courtroom.

As I stated earlier, there was no one from the defendant's family or friends in attendance. We assumed maybe it was the bad weather or the distance they had to travel or that no one believed a verdict would be reached so fast. I don't know why I was thinking about that but I found it sad that no one at all was there for the pair.

The jurors had the choice whether or not to stay after the verdict to speak to the family, and most did not. I would have liked to thank them all but I did not make it out of the courtroom in time. Sean told me he spoke to two of the female jurors just long enough for them to say how sorry they were. He said both ladies were crying as they spoke to him.

Some of the boys' friends left the courthouse to celebrate and invited us along. Riley and I just wanted to go home. It was going to take us a very long time to relax after the last two weeks. We were exhausted and just wanted to decompress.

I received an email the next day from a woman who, at that time, I had never met. She worked with Brandon at Hennessey's as a bartender. She felt she had something to say and gave me permission to add her email to my book.

Sent: Thursday, December 18, 2008 5:05 PM
Subject: A trial footnote clearing something up

Hi everyone, I received this email this morning from a friend and co-worker of Brandon's and I asked her if I could share it and she gladly agreed. It is a moot point now with the trial over but I was so thankful she wrote. Brahim made the decisions on the witnesses regarding that family's allegation against Brandon and it all turned out well as you know but it was nice to hear the side of someone else that was there and I know you all appreciate knowing what we know. Just so you can visualize it, a patio separates Hennessey's Tavern and the Fish Bucket. You can eat and drink on either side. So here it is... We so appreciate Sheila for writing!!!!

"You don't know me. My name is Sheila. I am one of the bartenders at the Bucket and worked with Whitey (our name for Brandon). I just now read all the emails about the trial and after being at the courtroom yesterday, I just want you to know that my prayers are with you and your family. I often think of Whitey especially working late nights. He was always there to make sure we were safe at the end of the night. I really miss him. I was just looking at his picture in the office last Sunday and I think of him as an angel still our protector.

This might be a bit late.....when I heard the defense attorney yesterday about the incident; I was there the night the fight broke out with the family. I was behind the bar with the manager on duty and two other bartenders. When the fight broke out I was trying to grab all the glassware from the bar and looked at one of the cocktail waitresses to get help and get all the bouncers because the family started to attack Herb. He was the only bouncer there at the time and the family attacked him and the guy bartenders. To make this short, Whitey was not even around and he did not now what was going on because he was next door at the tavern. I CLEARLY REMEMBER looking at Whitey from the inside bar as he walked through the patio towards the Bucket yell, "CALL THE COPS ALREADY!!!" I will never forget his facial expression that night. I even told him that night I had never seen him so frustrated. By the time the fight was out in the parking lot Whitey was trying to calm the situation down. Whitey never had anyone in a headlock!! He wasn't even in the fight. Whatever the family said and what the defense said was not true. I'm sorry this was late but, I didn't know this incident was even going to be brought up. I along with the 2 other bartenders would have testified on behalf of your son. Your son was a VERY GOOD MAN and he was very passionate about his job, very professional and always had that smile. Yes he was a big guy but, he was a gentle giant. I'm sorry this was a bit late but, I just wanted you to know the truth about this. Please know that I along with many other people think of Whitey and your family. Be strong." Sheila

Erin White

Accessory After the Fact

For her part in destroying evidence after the fact, Ms. Wilson could not have been happy with the guilty verdicts. As I stated before, if Kelley and Nelson's verdict had been not guilty, in the eyes of the law, there would have been no crime for Ms. Wilson to be accessory to.

Her trial date had previously been moved to the end of January 2009. Before that date came she had reached a plea deal. For destroying evidence, even after she knew that someone had been killed, she pled guilty and was sentenced to time served in county jail (I believe it ended up being 76 days), and probation. I, for one, would have very much liked to hear her story and rationale for what she did. For me, the fact that she knowingly destroyed evidence was a crime, whether or not Kelley and Nelson were found guilty.

There was one particular day that Riley and I could not be in attendance during one of the hearings. There was a motion to continue the trial date yet again. A friend of ours was in the courtroom that day. She recalled that Ms. Wilson was not happy that the date was being changed again. Our friend heard Ms. Wilson say that she wanted to "get on with her life." It disturbed me to hear of such words being said as Brandon would, I'm sure, have preferred to get on with his life too.

As I previously said, I would have liked to hear her story, but that was not to be. I will never know exactly why she did what she did. She was related to at least two of the people in the group. Her son was one of the eight who went to the Tavern that night and her niece, Ms. Fowler, was Kelley's girlfriend. Did she think she was protecting them? She knew someone died that night...

Sentencing Day, February 20th, 2009

As you will read in the following email from the formal sentencing of Kelley and Nelson there was quite a turn out in support of Brandon.

We were not quite sure what to expect but were amazed at the amount of security in the room, some in uniform and some in plain clothes. "Emotions run high and tempers can flair", we were told.

Victims assist Melissa said that although there was appropriate "trial wear" during the actual proceedings, at the sentencing, we could dress more casually. Anyone who wanted to could wear a commemorative t-shirt in Brandon's honor if they chose to.

Many wore the white ribbons that were handed out at the funeral. Most of his friends wore t-shirts that had been made over the last two years, some from the fundraisers, some green ones they all wore for St. Patrick's Day with his name on them. All of them memorialized Brandon in some way.

Colleen and some of the girls wore a shirt made in memory of the one-year anniversary of his death. It was white and said across the top "We miss you Whitey." On the back of the shirt were angel wings with a big "B" in the middle.

In Brandon's honor, Sean, Josh, Patrick, Jerod, Herb and a few others wore pea coats with the white ribbon pinned to them. Seems quite a few of the guys have those coats and I thought they looked really great. Brandon had one as well, his fathers from his Navy days.

My friend Deb made me a special t-shirt. On her computer she put together a collage of pictures of Brandon and the result was ironed on to a shirt I bought ahead of time. It was so cool! I loved it! I was proud to wear it that day.

As we entered the courtroom, none of us knew what the outcome would be. I had been constantly worried over the last two weeks and this day was no exception. The fate of the two men was to be decided. I wasn't sure how I felt. For one thing, I was nervous about reading my impact statement in front of so many. I had printed my letter in a very large sized font so I would not get lost and might be able to look up occasionally. I also put each page in a plastic cover and bound them together. Knowing I would be anxious, I was not taking any chances of losing my place.

When it became clear that the trial was eminent anyone who wanted to was encouraged to write a letter (an impact letter) on Brandon's behalf. These letters were addressed to the judge directly. All the letters are kept in a permanent file and anytime the defendant's files are opened, the letters are there. My friend Karen had been through the trial process recently, following the murder of her son. She encouraged me to include pictures of Brandon along with my letter. Not only would there be letters upon letters in this file but also a face to go along with those letters.

Impact statements are letters written and read directly to the judge on sentencing day, prior to the actual sentencing. It is your opportunity to say how Brandon's loss had affected you personally. You do not look at the defendants when speaking, only at the judge. Usually only family members of the victim actually read their statements in the courtroom. On TV it always appeared that the statements were directed to the guilty parties, but that is not how it really was, at least not for us. I wondered if it was the judge's decision to direct the statements to him. I know Kelley and Nelson had to listen, and I would have loved to speak directly to them. That was not the protocol.

I have included a copy of my impact statement as well as Colleen's and Sean's exactly as we wrote them and exactly as they were read in the courtroom. Riley wrote an impact statement, which I have included, although he chose not to read his aloud. He did not think he could read it and keep control of his emotions.

Judge Fasel
Superior Court, County of Orange,
Case #07ZF0004

RE: Sentencing of (Kelley & Nelson)

To the honorable Judge Fasel,

My name is Erin White. Brandon Alexander White was and is my son.

How can a mother possibly sum up her son in a few short paragraphs? How can a mother be asked to bury her son, her second born, her baby boy.

On January 1, 2007 the actions of the 2 defendants forever changed our family. Brandon's murder robbed the world of a wonderful man, a loyal friend and our beloved child. Robbed the world of a brother, grandson, nephew and cousin. Stolen from Brandon, his life and his dreams, stolen from us, the knowledge that we would never experience the joy of seeing him grow to the man he was surely to become, never to see him married and having children. Brandon worked two jobs and attended Cal State Fullerton majoring in Criminal Justice. His goal was to become an Orange County Sheriff, to protect and serve. A dream shattered by the violent actions the defendants.

That night of January 1, 2007 at the hospital I was not even allowed to see him. He was "evidence" I was told. I felt my heart had been ripped from my body that I could not see my son. I felt that being able to see him would have made it more real to me. These two men even stole that from me.

Brandon was a wonderful baby and the best sleeper of the three. He loved his momma and as a child he always asked for me to sing the song "Inch Worm" at bedtime. He would change the words at the end of the song to instead of "seems to me you'd stop and see how beautiful they are" referring to the marigolds in the song, he would sing" seems to me you'd stop and see how beautiful mommy is". My heart would swell every time. Brandon's favorite Christmas would have to be the one where we got him a Little Tykes "Cozy Coop." He was around the age of 4. It was bright yellow and red and you got in it and using your feet could "drive' all over. He loved that thing and didn't want to get out!

Brandon played soccer and flag football as a child and then football in high school and college. In high school he played both offense and defense and made Varsity his sophomore year. Nothing was more fun than hearing your sons name over the loud speaker when he had made a tackle. We could often hear his "roar" on the sidelines as he tried to get the team pumped up. He was the recipient of the "Charger Pride Award" in high school. An honor earned by nomination from a teacher. This award is given to a student who demonstrates dependability, character strength, honesty, maturity and integrity. He was all of those and more.

When Brandon wanted his hair cut his dad would take him in the garage and with much difficulty would shave Brandon's head. His hair was thick so this was no easy task. In return Brandon was to clean up after and sweep. Recently we had to replace our dryer and found that yes, Brandon had done as he was told but had swept all the hair under the dryer every time his dad cut his hair. There we found mounds of his thick red hair! I laughed and cried at the same time.

Brandon was a "gentle giant". I have been told over and over how safe he made the people around him feel. He was such a presence in a room. He was a positive role model and a gentleman. I am told he always made sure the girls got safely to their cars at the end of a shift. Brandon was a kind, caring, wonderful man and I was so proud of him.

Thru his wonderful friends whom we love so much we have learned so much more about our son. We have been able to see him through their eyes. His friends meant everything to him. We have bouncer BBQ's, gatherings at our home to enjoy their company and share stories. The adult Brandon we often saw was the tired, hungry Brandon, who opened the front door and said "hey", ate something, threw himself on the couch and promptly fell asleep.

Brandon loved to hang out with his brother Sean. They shared a room for 18 years, were best friends as well as brothers. On Christmas Eve they would take wrapping paper and lock them selves in their room and laugh and laugh. We would wonder what they were doing in there. On Christmas morning we would receive gifts "disguised" in boxes wrapped with magazines and T-shirts and socks and videos. Brandon loved to irritate his sister Colleen and she did a good job of irritating him right back. But she knew he would be right there if she needed him, and he was.

Brandon was also very proud of his Nordic heritage! But Brandon loved his family and his friends above all. There was nothing he would not do for someone else. No one he wouldn't help move to a new place or motivate to be better. He was polite and kind and careful with his money. He did, however love wearing nice clothes, loved his noisy black truck, loved to go paint balling with a group of guys, loved sushi, loved a good cigar, loved his dads special spare ribs and my chicken enchilada's and meatloaf. He loved cherries and loved Henry Weinhards Vanilla Cream Soda. His favorite beer was New Castle and favorite cookies were Samoa's Girl Scout Cookies! A couple of favorite movies were Monsters Inc. and the 13th Warrior. He loved the silver ring his dad gave him and wore it all the time and oh, he loved his rainbows!

I spoke with him that night of January 1st. Exactly at midnight as we always did. I told him I loved him and that I would see him tomorrow to hang out and watch football. He said he loved me too and that he would see me tomorrow. Tomorrow never came for us. We kept Brandon's cell phone on long after he was gone so that we could hear his voice when the days get so dark for us. Be assured that his cell phone got many calls not just from us but also from the countless others who share our grief and loss.

I miss my son every minute of every day. I miss his beautiful red hair, his deep infectious laugh, his gorgeous smile and his wonderful voice. I miss the smell of his cologne. Brandon and I shared a mutual love for all kinds of music. We would sit on the couch and listen to music and our heads would bob in unison to songs like "Blue on Black" by Kenny Wayne Shepard and "Enter Sandman" by Metallica. Brandon also loved classical music and would often study while listening to Mozart and Andrea Bocelli. He would also indulge me and listen to Journey and Whitesnake.

To know that Brandon suffered pain that night and the knowledge that I was not there to comfort and help him is unbearable. Two others were hurt that night, physically and emotionally and live daily with the reminder of what happened to them and to their friend.

In Brandon's truck we found his bible marked at Matthew 5:9 "blessed are the peacemaker's. We have all sort of adopted that scripture and in fact I have those words forever on my body along with a portrait tattoo of my son. Brandon will always have my back!

Brandon, "B", Bran, Brenda (as Sean called him when he wanted to make him mad), and "Whitey" as all his friends called him. All endearments for a man this world must to do without.

I hope that the defendants remember every day the pain they have caused our family. The pain they have caused their own families. A kind of pain there is no cure for and no relief from.

It is my wish is that the two defendants are sentenced to the full extent that the law will allow.

Thank you, Erin White

Judge Fasel
Superior Court, County of Orange,
Case #07ZF0004
RE: Sentencing of (Kelley & Nelson)

Your Honor:
My name is Riley White. Brandon White is my son.

How does a father explain the impact at the loss of a son? How do you measure the pain, the sense of lost, and the outrage over the waste?

When I pulled up to the ER that morning, I saw the EMT and a nurse trying to clean up all the blood. I spent four years as a Navy Corpsman, one of which was with the Marines, I knew what that much blood would mean and I knew my world and my family would never be the same. When Brandon was just moments old, he held on to my finger with his little hand. Twenty-one years later I held his hand while he lay in his coffin. NO FATHER SHOULD EVER HAVE TO BURY HIS CHILD, EVER!

My son was an interesting young man. On the outside he looked like the typical football jock, big and strong with a look that could freeze you but on the inside was a deep, thoughtful man, and caring man, mature beyond his years, a born leader that the Bouncers, even the older ones, knew they could trust to calm a bad situation. Unlike the thug he was portrayed, as by the defense, Brandon was more interested in calming a situation without conflict then creating one. In his cell phone I found a half a dozen taxi company telephone numbers he would use to call rides for the customers who he knew shouldn't drive, and more then a few times he paid for the rides out of his own pocket. The Deputy Sheriffs in the South County that came into contact with Brandon at Hennessey's and the Tavern saw those traits in Brandon and wanted him on their team and he wanted to be one of the "good guys", as he would say.

Following his murder, Hennessey's had two memorials for him and at both, people came up to me to say what Brandon meant to them, story after story by people he had touched and, in many cases, changed their lives. There were nearly six hundred people attending Brandon's funeral, doctors, teachers, coaches, teammates from football, Deputy's, friends, family, and strangers (to us) who knew my son and felt the loss as much as we, all this for a 21 year old man.

I will never know how Brandon would have turned out, I'll never see him wear that green uniform, or hold his children. All of that was taken from us by the act of a coward. After two years, the sorrow is still deep and anger still intense. I miss my son. This is the last act I can do as a father for his lost son. Your Honor, on behalf of Brandon and on behalf of his family and friends, I ask that you sentence those responsible for his murder to the maximum length of time provided for by law. So no other father will have to hear that his son has been killed.

Judge Fasel
Superior Court, County of Orange,
Case #07ZF0004
RE: Sentencing of (Kelley & Nelson)

To the honorable Judge Fasel,
My name is Sean White. Brandon Alexander White was and is my Brother.
On January 1st, 2007 my brother Brandon was murdered. The actions of the two defendants have forever changed me, changed my family and our many friends. Because of them I have lost my brother and best friend. Because of them the world has lost a man who always thought of others first and himself second. He worked hard in life so he could succeed. All he wanted to do was protect the people around him. He was going to school and hoped to become an Orange County Sheriff. He had dreams and goals. Now his dreams and goals are lost forever.
I will never forget the night of Jan 1st. I was at a New Year's party right up the street from Timeout Tavern. I was even going to go there to wish him a happy New Year in person. Then I got the call from my mom saying that Brandon was hurt and taken to the hospital. At first I didn't think much about it because I had taken him there before when a patron bit him. As I was driving it was the weirdest thing because I felt like there was something wrong. When I got to the ER I will never forget the first thing I saw and was the ambulance being hosed down because of all the blood that was lost. Then In the ER I was met by about 50 people and many of them I had never seen before. When I was told the news I broke down and the rest of that week was so surreal.

Brandon was my younger brother and he I shared a room for about 18 years. He and I had a lot of good times growing up, he always liked to tail around with me growing up because he wanted to be cool and hangout with the older kids. One of my best memories was when I was a senior in high school and he was a sophomore. We were playing Trabuco Hills High School and we were beating them pretty good so the coaches put in Brandon so he could get some playing time. I played defensive end and he played defensive tackle. He got in and I remember looking at him in the huddle and his eyes were huge. I just told him to take a breath and hit hard. That play they ran to our side and we both converged on the tackle and the stadium announcer called out "Tackle made by White and White."

There are so many good memories of Brandon that I would love to tell but there isn't enough time. Brandon and I were very close, he was my best friend and because of the actions of these two men on January 1st he is gone. I have lost my brother, my sister has lost her brother and my parents have lost their little boy. Who knows what he could have done and or be but we will never know now.

I hope that the defendants get sentenced to the full extent of the law. I also hope that when they sit in there cells they think of what they have done to my family and friends for the thoughtless act that they committed. They will never be forgiven.

Thank you, Sean White

Judge Fasel
Superior Court, County of Orange,
Case #07ZF0004
RE: Sentencing of (Kelley & Nelson)

To the honorable Judge Fasel

My name is Colleen White. Brandon White was my brother. Brandon was a great big brother and I have some memories that stand out in my mind that I would like to share.

I was staying home alone over night for the first time. My parents went out of town for the weekend and they said I was old enough to stay home alone so I was really excited. I was sitting in our living room and it had to be around midnight and I kept hearing all these sounds out side and I started getting really scared. I thought there was someone out there. I called Brandon because I knew he would answer his phone. He answered and asked me if everything was ok and I told him I kept hearing noises out side and I didn't know what to do. He told me to go turn on all the lights, lock all the doors and windows get all the phones in the house and grab a flashlight and call him back. I did what he told me and then called him back. Brandon was either out with friends or at work at the time but he stayed on the phone with me until I felt safe. I hung up with him and everything was fine. He called me about 20 minutes later just to check up on me and to make sure I was doing ok. I will never forget what he did.

Another one of my memories is when Brandon took me out to eat sushi for the first time. He made me try all different kinds and he would not let me spit it out. He kept saying "Colleen, just swallow it." That was probably one of the best times I had with him. On the ride home we started talking about me going to college and what I wanted to major in. I kept telling him I had no clue what to major in but he would not drop the subject. The one thing I remember about when we were talking was he that told me "Never let anyone tell you that you can't do it. Prove them wrong and keep going for what you want, because you're a Whitey and Whitey's never give up!"

That's what made Brandon such a great brother. We may have fought and picked on each other but I guess that's just what big brothers and little sisters do but he would always protect me. He would always put other people before himself. He would always do things with out complaining.

The thing that will always make me the saddest is that after all the good advise he gave me about following my dreams and doing well in school Brandon never got to see his own sister graduate from high school. Will never get to see me get married or see his brother coach in his first football game or even take another family tattoo picture.

As we look into the future or right now for that matter all we have left of Brandon is remembering his wonderful personality, his heart of gold, and the great memories that I will hold onto forever

Thank you, Colleen White

I have included my email from the evening after we heard the verdict.

Sent: Fri, 20 Feb 2009 6:18 pm

Subject: Sentencing update, the wait is over

Hello all,

First I must thank all of you for the love and support. I know I have said it over and over but we truly would not have been able to get thru this with out each and every one of you. We are so thankful to everyone. Today was to be a 2-hour process but was not. We were all there early, about 60 of us we are told to meet with DA Brahim in the conference room. Brahim told us what was to go on and that there would be a large police presence in uniform and plain clothes and to conduct ourselves as we always did. We were in the courtroom at 9 and were all still waiting at 10:30. Seems Kelley had not been transported yet among other things. Friday's in the courtroom are reserved for things like ours and motions etc. There were 2 other cases that had quick motions regarding continuances (we know about those) and then by 11am it was our turn. Kelley as you heard filed a motion to get a new attorney and trial. It was very tense for us all week. While Brahim was "cautiously optimistic" it would not fly there is always that worry. The judge denied the motion and before the words were out of his mouth Kelley blurted out that he wanted a "Marsden" (sp) hearing. He is not supposed to speak out like that I don't think but did anyway. We believe that this Marsden hearing may have been something Kelley learned of in jail as a last resort and as a way to fire his lawyer and the judge cannot deny this conversation. Judge Fasel did not seem happy. We were all sent out of the courtroom, as this is a closed discussion between the judge and Kelley. More tense moments as everyone waited outside. Even Brahim waited with us.

The moments wore on and I wondered if that was bad. Brahim assured me that quick or slow he did not feel the judge would grant it.

After 20 minutes or so we were all called in. Without discussing the conversation with Kelley the sentencing started. I read my impact statement, which is read directly to the judge. The love in the room and the fact that judge looked right at me the whole time helped me through what was one of the hardest things I have ever done. Sean and Colleen also spoke. The sentences were read and are very confusing but as we understand it Kelley was given 71 years to life (the 1 is because of the use of the knife as the weapon). He will not be eligible for parole until 71 years have passed and Brahim says they do not grant parole usually in a murder case. Nelson was given 32 years to life and no eligibility for parole for 32 years. Again unlikely either man will ever get out of prison. They may file appeal but that takes years.

I have added an email from Victims assistant Melissa regarding everyone's conduct in the courtroom today. "Mama Bear", (a pet name for me from the bouncers) had told everyone attending they must behave and they did that and more. I am so proud that all kept their cool on what was an emotional day and all throughout the trial. The OC register reporter was there and I gave him my impact statement and said he could use what he liked in his story. It should be in the paper and online under the local section. He is a nice man and was there throughout.

Ok, I will let you know as soon as we are told were the 2 will go to prison and here is what Melissa said. Love to all,

Erin

"Let everyone know that they were extremely respectful of the court! A few investigators came up to me in shock of the amount of people that showed up today and asked if I was okay with all these people. I told them I was confident there would not be any problems (past sentencings haven't gone as smoothly, I guess???) And thank you and all your family for being so patient with today's proceedings!!! The delay was truly unexpected but not once did I hear anyone complain or get upset. You guys are such a loving and supportive family and it truly saddens me that this had to happen to such good people. Take good care and talk to you soon!"

I wanted to explain what I found out later regarding a Marsden Hearing. If a defendant feels the public defender appointed is not working in their best interest, a request can be made that new counsel be selected.

Kelley had first asked to continue or delay sentencing so that he could hire a private attorney. My understanding was that he could not show proof to the judge that other counsel had been retained. It was after the denial of his request for more time that he shouted out that he wanted a Marsden Hearing. We think he may have heard about a Marsden hearing from another inmate while detained in county jail. After his outburst, the bailiffs seemed startled and immediately moved closer to him.

In most jurisdictions a "Marsden Hearing" is permitted. This hearing allows the court to listen to the defendant's specific concerns.

However, you must show the court that there is a serious problem. This complaint is usually done in letterform to the judge first, requesting a meeting with him regarding your dissatisfaction. A copy of the letter is sent to both the defense and prosecuting attorneys. I later found out that a formal letter is not always necessary and the DA does not have to be informed ahead of time. In our case, Brahim was unaware.

Kelley's request was granted but the judge did not seem happy about the delay in sentencing. A Marsden hearing is a closed hearing, and we were sent out of the courtroom. All who remained, as far we know, was Kelley, his attorney and the judge. As I stated in my email, even Brahim was not in the courtroom for this meeting. I wondered if the transcriber was present and if what transpired in that meeting was recorded? It must have been, but I did not see any of it in the transcripts.

It was a very nervous time for all of us. Brahim explained to all of us what was happening. We had to stand outside the courtroom and wait for however long it took.

We were told, after a time (it was at least 20 minutes or more), to return to our seats and after everyone was again seated the judge gave the sentences to both men. No mention was made of the meeting between the judge and Kelley. I assumed, and so did everyone with us, that Kelley's motion was not granted. I have to admit I found it strange that the judge did not even bring up any of it. The Marsden hearing and its results were confidential, I guess.

I will also break down the sentencing to make it clearer.

Defendant Kelley for the murder of Brandon was sentenced to 25 years to life. Because he had a prior strike or felony, the sentence was doubled to 50 years to life. For the use of a knife during the murder of Brandon he got an additional year. Because he had a prior serious felony, he got an additional 5 years. The total sentence for Brandon's murder is 56 years to life.

For the attempted murder of Steve, Kelley got 7 years to life. Because of the prior strike, the sentence was doubled to 14 years to life. Due to the use of the knife during attempted murder of Steve, he got an additional year. His total sentence for attempted murder of Steve is 15 years to life.

Since Judge Fasel made the decision to run the sentences consecutive to each other rather than concurrently the total sentence was 71 years to life. That meant that he would not have the option petition the state parole board until after he has served 71 years in prison.

Defendant Nelson, found guilty in Brandon's murder was sentenced to 25 years to life. He had no prior felony on his record; therefore the sentence was not doubled as it was for Kelley. For the attempted murder of Steve his total sentence was 7 years to life. Again, the judge's decision was to run his sentences consecutively to each other, defendant Nelson's total sentence is 32 years to life.

We were told that the District Attorney's office has a policy of opposing release of defendants convicted of murder. Parole, the first time they are eligible to request it, typically is not granted.

I cannot say what we expected as far as the sentencing. Knowing the men responsible for our son's death would answer for their crimes, be unable to hurt anyone else and would go to prison, was a relief. Our family had asked that both men receive the maximum sentences allowed by law and that was exactly what happened.

On my way out of the courtroom, I again stopped to talk to reporter Larry Welborn. He asked for a statement from me regarding the sentencing. I said that I was "happy justice was served for Brandon and Steve". I handed over my impact statement and told Larry he could use what he wanted to from it. He did utilize part some of what I said in the article about the sentencing that appeared in the next days newspaper. I also stopped to thank the two bailiffs that were with us every day. I hugged them and they both said how sorry they were.

Riley recalled walking past me and out of the courtroom. He and quite a few people including Sean, Steve and several of the bouncers and friends stood in a large group talking. A woman he believed was Kelley's half sister (she had been a frequent attendee, so he is fairly sure) said, as she waited for the elevator, and loud enough for all to hear, "My brother will probably die in prison because of Brandon White." Riley said everyone looked at her very strangely in shock and disbelief. Colleen heard her and was visibly upset by her words. I asked Riley later why no one responded to her outburst and he replied that everyone that heard it was too stunned at the time and then she was gone.

The sentencing did not bring me any joy and in fact even Judge Fasel said that not only did our family lose Brandon, both the defendants families had in a way, lost their sons as well. A sobering thought

After Trial Barbeque, at Our House

The Saturday after the February 20, 2009, sentencing we hosted yet another get-together at our house. This "bouncer" barbeque marked what was the end of a very long passage in all of our lives.

On a personal level it was our family's opportunity to gather together all those who had been so supportive to us during such an extremely stressful, nerve-wracking and emotional time. So many gave up so much to sit by our sides in that courtroom day after day.

I have written over and over about Brandon's loyalty to his friends. I must tell you now that the loyalty every one of them showed to him everyday by being present in that room with us is something I will never forget.

I had been beating myself up (metaphorically, of course), feeling that I had not celebrated Brandon's life. I wondered if I appeared as gloomy as I felt. This particular barbeque was a CELEBRATION!

We were all happy that day. Happy to have many people we loved together in one place, happy the trial was over; happy justice had been served for our son. This barbeque gave us all a chance to enjoy each other's company, share a meal and even a few laughs. Joe Gaul even stopped by making the whole event even more memorable.

During that evening, Brandon's friend Rob took Riley aside and gave him a very special gift. Rob was a friend, as well as a fellow bouncer. He had been on duty as security at the Tavern the night Brandon died. Rob is a Sergeant First Class in the Army (Special Forces). Rob had done several tours including Bosnia, Iraq and Afghanistan. It was on a tour in Iraq that he earned two Bronze Stars. The Bronze Star is a medal given for bravery.

Rob handed Riley a blue case. Inside the case, embedded in velvet, was one of his Bronze Stars. Here was a man who had served his country "above and beyond the call of duty." With mist in his eyes, he said that he wanted us to have one of his medals because he felt Brandon had been, "braver than he could ever be."

By this time Riley had motioned me over to join the two of them. Riley and I were both so moved by Rob's announcement we could not speak. He went on to say that the other Bronze Star was buried in Iraq and someday when someone dug it up they would know "we" America had been there.

To see such a wonderful man having been awarded for bravery, so emotional over the loss of his friend, is something that will forever stick in my mind. Rob sharing his medal with us was a very poignant moment and truly beyond words.

That night we were yet again surrounded by love and I have to say it felt really good. I could not help but think what a lucky guy Brandon was to have them all in his life and how lucky we are to have them in ours.

Post Trial

It took us several weeks to sort of "come down" from all that had happened during the trial. It felt almost anti-climactic actually.

For almost two years, all we thought about was how devastated we were by Brandon's loss, when the trial would be, and when the people responsible for taking our son from us would answer for their crimes.

I was told our feelings were natural, but we thought, "what now?"

The trial and what might happen in that courtroom had been uppermost in our minds for so long. We had bonded with Brahim, Joe Gaul and Victims Assistant Melissa. Although we had never met any of them prior to Brandon's murder, we had been in regular contact for two years, by phone, email or in person at hearings and motions. During the trial, we saw and talked to them daily.

All three know our family's depth of feeling for them. For me, it was a very bittersweet parting. I knew they all must move forward with other cases, other families and other tragedies. Brahim, Joe and Melissa will always have a piece of my heart and our whole family's undying gratitude not only for the excellent way they represented Brandon but for their friendship as well.

If I heard this comment once, I heard it a million times. "Well, now with the end of the trial at least you have closure." The pain of Brandon's death hurts as badly at this second as it did that first second. Closure? No.

I think, at first, your thoughts rarely stray from your sadness. I found I could not think of much else. As time passes though, your heart is still heavy, but your mind does wander away to other things. However, it is not difficult to fall in to a downhearted mood. For me, hearing a song we both liked, cooking a meal I know he loved or spending another holiday with out him brings up to the surface such feelings of how very much his loss still effects my daily life.

Christmas and New Year's are the hardest for me. When writing out our Christmas cards, I continually make the mistake of signing the card, Love from, Erin, Riley, Sean, Brandon and Colleen. I have to catch myself and really think about not putting his name in. It seems so natural to do so. Christmas, a holiday I love above all, is a sad reminder that we will not be together as a complete family ever again. The professional portrait the kids do for me each year as a Christmas gift is missing his smiling face. I know getting the picture taken is not as much fun for Colleen and Sean without Brandon, but they still it to please me. Decorating for Christmas is often bittersweet, especially when we find an ornament or gift made lovingly by Brandon when he was young. Often the emotion hits you like a ton of bricks and gives you no warning.

New Year's Day, for obvious reasons is a day Riley and I, for lack of a better word, dread. Sure, all other holidays remind us of our loss, but that day is the worst. We spend New Year's Eve with friends, usually Liz and Steve and Denise and Joe, the same couples we were with the night he died. We are so glad to have a few hours to take our mind off the inevitable, overwhelming depression the next day brings. New Year's Day is always spent quietly at home and includes a visit to the gravesite as a family.

On January 1st, 2008, the first anniversary of Brandon's death, many including members of both sides of our families, friends, bouncers and Pastor Greg met at the gravesite. Pastor Greg spoke and we all prayed together. Anyone who wanted to shared a memory of Brandon with the group. While New Year's Day is typically a big day for visitors to his site, there is no organized time usually.

This last New Year's Day we arrived at the cemetery and were greeted by several of Brandon's friends who, as if by magic, chose the very same time to stop over. It had rained recently so I brought granite cleaner and a toothbrush (a toothbrush works well on getting dirt out of the grooves in the lettering) to clean up the headstone. Molly had a similar thought and also had water and a toothbrush with her. We all not only had a great visit, but left everything sparkling!

Brandon's birthday is another tough day. He is not here to celebrate it. I become very melancholy thinking, "he would be 22 this year" or 23, 24, 25. The occasional piece of mail addressed to him is still delivered to our house. My heart hurts to know I cannot save it on the counter for the next time he stops by.

I can say, in a sense, the conclusion of the trial was the end of a very long chapter in our lives. A chapter filled with highs and lows, disappointment and triumph, emotion and tears, and yes, justice.

Erin White

Justice for a good boy who grew to be a good man, both cherished and admired. A man we were so very proud of, a man who wanted to make something of his life through education and career choice. Brandon had a gift for making people feel safe and secure and an instinct for protecting those who could not protect themselves. To say that our lives are not complete without him is an understatement.

Forgiveness, is it Possible?

I visit and help care for my mom on Friday's with rare exception. Recently, she asked me that very question. "Honey do you think you can ever forgive them?"

"Mom, I'm not sure", was my hasty answer. She did not press me and I could not bring myself to ask her if she would be able to forgive such an act against one of her children. Could any of my friends or family forgive the heartbreak of murder against one of theirs?

I have thought about the word forgiveness endlessly. For me, if the defendants had shown any sort of torment or anguish over what had happened to Brandon, to our family, to our lives, I think my mind and my heart might feel differently.

Kelley claimed that he acted in self-defense, which the jury obviously did not believe. Never in his eyes, testimony or body language did I ever see any sign that he was sorry, in fact, he showed little reaction at all. He murdered our son and never did I see much feeling whatsoever. Only when he was sentenced did he show any reaction.

Nelson was convinced he would be found innocent. Even though the law regarding his involvement had to have been explained in detail to him, he never seemed contrite. His actions that night aggravated the situation and, as a result, Kelley pulled a knife and stabbed Brandon and slashed Steve. I will always wonder why Nelson wasn't furious with his friend for all the trouble he got him into.

I was raised to forgive. It was just what my parents believed and what we were taught. These men took the life of our son. Colleen and Sean lost their brother. How does one begin to feel forgiveness? I have had to get over my own feelings of guilt because I cannot in my heart forgive them. You might be thinking that I have to be the better person and forgive. Or you might be thinking that what they did was unforgivable. Will I, one day, be able to forgive, I cannot say. Forget what they did, never!

While getting ready for work one morning the news was on the TV in our bedroom. I was drawn to the story of a man who was being interviewed about the murder of his daughter. His words struck me so I quickly jotted them down.

He said that he felt forgiveness was "a tool for healing." "Forgiveness was not a journey but a path." I thought a lot about his words.

A "tool for healing", I wondered if he was saying that I needed to attempt to heal myself and heal my own heart. It may not be about Kelley or Nelson and their lack of remorse at all.

In talking with friends and family there are varying opinions on the subject of forgiveness. The one thing I know is that if forgiveness of some sort is possible, it has to happen in my own time.

I think I have spent more time reflecting about this section in my book than any other. I have put un-due pressure on myself to feel something that I just cannot feel. Brandon's life was ended because of a horrible decision of another. Where do I begin to feel anything but pain?

My girlfriend Billie told me "un-forgiveness keeps me stuck." That forgiveness is part of healing (seems to be a common feeling). She said that I couldn't control how the defendant thinks or how he reacts or doesn't react. The only thing I have control over is me. She went on to say that God forgives us and He also knows that for us to experience life to the fullest, we need to forgive others. "This is much easier said than done", she added, and it would not happen over night. It is a process. I was touched by her words and have thought about them a great deal.

My friend Liz told me that Brandon's murder was a "scar that will never go away." Some days the emotion is so raw that I feel that scar gets ripped wide open.

Even as I write this, I am of two minds. I understand and appreciate all the wonderful words of love and encouragement I get. This is not something that one day you wake up and the sun is shining and the birds are singing and you feel forgiveness. At least, I do not believe it will be that way for me.

Karen, who lost her son Jason in a similar and violent way, suggested that maybe I was confusing forgiving with forgetting. I might somehow feel guilt that by forgiving I will not honor Brandon. While I have not consciously thought that, it gave me something to think about. I know to forgive or not must be something I do in my own time. She of all people understands that.

Karen said she tries to think of what her son would want for her and that would be peace. I know that Brandon would want the same for me. I will continue to strive to find that peace within my self. The rational part of me says that I must find it. The emotional part of me says unless that you have experienced such a loss you can only imagine, in your worst dreams, how it feels.

I must walk my own road and in my own time. There was no limit in my capacity of love for Brandon. Forgiveness is a feeling, you can't touch it or will yourself to experience it. If the passage of time finds me at a crossroads, my heart will guide me. The light of my love for Brandon will never dim. It glows a hundred times a day because that is how often I think of him.

Maybe forgiveness is a willingness to let God place judgment and will come to these men after they leave this earth. The hate and bitterness I hold in my heart only hurts me. Sadly I fear I am not ready to let go of those feelings just yet. As I write the tears flow. I ask myself, why must life be so unfair?

Epilogue

As I write this, three years have passed since Brandon's life was taken. To us it feels more like three seconds! It took a celebrity speaking on TV about the untimely death of pop star Michael Jackson to make me think even more about celebrating a life that ended too soon.

Just the word, celebrate makes one think of happy times and I certainly did not feel I could ever again be in a place to feel real happiness. Celebrate can also mean to commemorate or to honor. My hope is that I have honored Brandon, in my writing and in many other ways I did not initially realize.

I, for one was over taken by the enormity of our loss. It enveloped me in a sadness that was like a window so smudged and dirty you could not see through it or past it.

The gentleman on TV, when he spoke about Michael Jackson said "we should not grieve too long; we should celebrate what he brought to the world of music and entertainment."

The first thing that popped into my head was "yeah it's easy for you to sit there and say not to grieve too long." How long is too long? Our loss is felt so deeply that the passage of time has done nothing to diminish it, only perhaps, to soften it.

However, as I listened to this man speak; I thought about Brandon and what he brought to the world. What he brought to his world, to our world and the world of every person he touched with his love and friendship.

The fact that Brandon is not on this earth anymore has caused a pain in my heart that there is no relief from and no cure for. However, I did take to heart what that gentleman said. I have tried hard not to dwell as much on how sad I am, but how my son, in a positive way, affected the life of every person he came in contact with, every person he called friend. There are even those who shared with me they truly believe that their lives were saved by his kindness, actions and words of encouragement.

I visited the gravesite today. I usually go once a week to make sure everything looks nice, using granite cleaner to shine up the headstone or water the flowers that are always there. I really don't have to worry; the grounds keepers do a lovely job. They know who we are now, know who Brandon was, and I feel, take extra special care. Riley goes almost every day. Once a week he picks up everything before the grounds are mowed then returns it the next day.

Blowing softly in the breeze is a garden flag that we change out seasonally or replace with a birthday flag during the month of May. Right now a USC Trojan football flag is at Brandon's gravesite and will remain through the football season. USC has always been our family's favorite college football team. A wooden cross Regan bought as well as several other personal items are always placed by his marker. Sometimes we arrive to find two bottles of New Castle beer, one full and one empty, as if whoever had visited had, in their way, shared a drink with their friend. Sometimes there might be a personal note tucked in a flowerpot from a friend who stopped by or from a stranger who wanted to share with us how Brandon touched their life.

As I drove home from the cemetery I tried to figure out what it is that draws me there. I know that the warm, caring, living Brandon is not there. Only his body buried deep in the ground. But, it is all I have. It is the closest I can get to him, ever, physically anyway. So I go, and I sit there for a few minutes and put my hand on the grass above where his body is. Some times I quietly say, "Hi Bran".

I gaze over the beautiful grounds of the cemetery and all around me is a sea of flowers. So many people buried there, all with a different story and all so very missed by loved ones.

I think Brandon would be proud of my book. I think he would wonder why I thought he was important enough to write about. I know that if he had it to do over he still would have intervened at the bar that night, always trying to protect those around him and keep them safe. While that does little to comfort me, it is who Brandon was.

As far as I know, few, if any of Brandon's closest circle of friends are bouncers anymore. Most stopped bouncing the night he was murdered or soon after. For that, I am happy. Being a bouncer can be a dangerous job, as our family discovered first hand.

Steve is just about to finish college with a Bachelor's degree in Communication with a plan to continue on and get his Masters. While his jaw bears a vivid scar, a sad token from that night, he has worked hard for his education and I am so proud of him. I asked Steve very recently if he would ever consider having the scar minimized by laser and he said "No." He wants to leave it the way it is as a reminder. He told me that when asked about his scar, no one believes him when he tells how he got it. Steve had a very hard time after Brandon's death. Holding Brandon in his arms as he lay dying was a life changing experience. Steve is a wonderful man and has a great future ahead and we consider him part of our family and love him dearly.

Herb was also affected deeply by Brandon's death, both physically and emotionally. After many failed surgeries (at least five I think) to try and re-attach the tendon severed in his index finger that night, he decided he is "done" and that finger will forever be damaged and in a permanent "hook" position. Herb, like Steve has already earned a Bachelor's degree. Originally Herb's major was Criminal Justice. He has since changed his major to Environmental Science and plans to graduate in December of 2010 with a Masters of Science in Environmental Studies with an emphasis in planning. According to his mom Laura, the possible reason for the change in majors was due to his experience the night Brandon was killed. The occurrence turned him off to possibly having to dealing with unreasonable and sometimes violent people day in and day out. I am also so happy to say that Herb and the beautiful Melissa are engaged and will be married in October of 2010. We are so excited for the both of them and by the time you read this they will be man and wife!

Regan has had a very hard time with Brandon gone. She felt that she needed a change and moved to New York about a year after he died. She was very successful as a sales assistant in a brokerage firm and in fact has a Broker's license. She has since moved back to California and is currently working in a family real estate business with her father and brother and is in a serious relationship with a very nice man who I have had the pleasure to meet. Regan and I are in touch quite often, by phone, email or visits, and I am so glad she is doing well. Regan was "lost" for quite a while, we all were. I feel so much better knowing she has found happiness. She is a wonderful person and a valued friend.

Josh is doing well also. He is part of a family business and is director of data entry, advertising and marketing as well as managing a bar part time. He misses "Whitey" so much and has been such a comfort to us, in more ways than he knows. We are always so happy to see him and when we cannot be together, keep in touch by phone.

I have to say that all of Brandon's friends are doing well. In fact a couple of the guys are now "daddies". Brandon would have a good laugh over that, I am sure! We love getting together with all of them as much as we can and miss them when we are not together.

Kelley and Nelson both convicted for Brandon's murder went back to the Orange County jail system after the February 20th, 2009 sentencing and remained there until approximately April 2009. They were then sent to Wasco State Prison in Kern County, California. Wasco is where most California inmates go initially while they are processed, classified and evaluated. An inmate could remain there for up to six months while a decision was made as to where they would be permanently housed. There are many criteria involved in permanent placement. These include security level, bed space and program needs.

There is a classification scoring system to determine the level of custody for inmates. In California they are level 1 (minimum) to level 4 (maximum). Initially scores are based on the sentence. Other factors are considered as well that indicate their level of violence. Both inmates came into the prison system with a sentencing of "life-plus" so automatically had enough points to make them level 4. I have been told that over time they can lower those scores based on, among other things, actions and behavior but that level 4 inmates can never become level 1.

In the summer of 2009 both men were sent to separate maximum-security California state prisons. Kelley's MEPD (minimum eligible parole date) is 2066 and Nelson's is 2039. These dates reflect the soonest either can request parole and we understand it is unlikely parole would be granted. Kelley will be into his 90's before he will get out of prison. We are all relieved that they are now permanently housed. It is my understanding that they both get "yard time" every day but the majority of the day is spent in their cell. This restriction may change over time.

As for the four of us, Riley works very hard, misses Brandon immeasurably and loves his children (and me) tremendously and unconditionally. His voice catch's anytime he speaks of Brandon. Riley has been my savior and I know the pain of Brandon's death is with him every day. Sean has had his struggles with the loss of his brother. He continues to work and coach high school football and to say he misses Brandon is an understatement. They shared a bond that only brothers can, stories and jokes that only they knew. Colleen is in college now and is quite a lady and has a very nice boyfriend. She is sad that her brother Brandon will never see the woman she has become.

Never see her graduate college, get married or know that his fondest wish came true, that his sister did become less annoying!

As for me, I felt my life consisted of "just going through the motions," for a very long time. I eventually have come to realize that Brandon would want me to live life and not be sad all the time. Even when the days are the darkest, I try to remember that.

On a lighter note, I am happy to report that reading and enjoying a book is now possible. Even a fashion magazine might make its way into my shopping bag occasionally.

I did not intend to write a "how to" book that had all the answers on coping with loss, because I don't have them, nor do I think anyone else does either. We all struggle with loss at one time or another, family, friends, acquaintances. It is part of life. Rather, this book was intended to give you some insight into the most personal of all losses, that of your child. Whether by illness or violence, the sorrow and sense of despair is the same. We all handle loss differently, some by ignoring it and hoping the pain will go away some day. Or, living with it and allowing yourself to experience the soul and heart rending sorrow and feeling of loss by trying to understand what has happened and how to go on when going on seems the hardest choice of all.

I have tried to retell, to the best of my ability, the story of Brandon's life and death. It was not an easy thing to do and I would rather not have relived the most tormenting parts. I felt a deep need to let others know about Brandon and his loss. I used the word "loss" a lot and while I apologize for the repetition of the word, it is the center of my feelings.

Through Brandon's friends, I have been lucky to learn about what kind of man he had become in their eyes and the eyes of others. It is one gift that came out of this. But at the end of the day, when you are alone with your thoughts, the word and emotion always returns. Loss.

Sharing Brandon's story has been my tribute to him. I hope I have honored his memory by sharing the truth however difficult and painful.

In my way I have celebrated your life Brandon. I love you and will always love you. You are forever in my heart. Rest in Peace warrior!

Postscript

On December 10th 2010 I got a message on my cell phone from Brahim. In the message he said he needed to tell Riley and I something and he did not want us to hear it from anyone or anywhere else.

Riley and I knew that both Kelley and Nelson had appealed their convictions. I think it must be common practice, especially for a murder conviction. We had no idea how long that process might take or when the appeals would be heard.

Brahim continued on to say that the California Court of Appeals had "affirmed" or upheld the conviction of Kelley. In other words, Kelley's request for appeal had been denied and his conviction and sentence would stand. However, Nelson's conviction had been overturned. As I am listening to his message my jaw dropped in disbelief. I have since been in contact with Brahim and I will explain, to the best of my ability, what all of this meant.

The case against Nelson was conducted on two theories of aiding and abetting. The first was that Nelson aided and abetted the murder and attempted murder. The second was that Nelson aided and abetted an assault with a deadly weapon, a battery, an assault, or a challenge to fight, and the natural and probable consequences of each of those offenses was murder and attempted murder.

In my research I have found that, to prove a defendant is an accomplice, the California Supreme Court has stated that the prosecution must show that the defendant acted with knowledge of the criminal purpose of the perpetrator and with an intent or purpose either of committing, or of encouraging or facilitating commission of the offense. When the offense charged is a specific intent crime, the accomplice must share the specific intent of the perpetrator; this occurs when the accomplice knows the full extent of the perpetrators criminal purpose and gives aid or encouragement with the intent or purpose of facilitating the perpetrators commission of the crime. Confusing to say the least!

Nelson's main position for appeal stated that there was insufficient evidence that he was legally liable for Brandon's murder,

159

and insufficient evidence that he knew Kelley had a knife and that Kelley was going to use it.

In our minds the appeals court overturned Nelson's conviction based on lack of evidence of aiding and abetting as opposed to what he was convicted of which was the probable consequences of his actions.

It is hard to say how we felt about this news. Riley and I both believe that Nelson was that catalyst that night. If he had not initiated combative behavior and continued to act in an aggressive manner but instead had gotten in the car and left as he was urged to do by the bouncers, Brandon might still be alive. We know it was Kelley who stabbed Brandon, but Nelson, by his actions and his words, bears responsibility for escalating the argument. Did Nelson know about Kelley's knife? Brahim believed it; investigator Joe believed it, as did the 12 jurors.

Initially I wondered whether Nelson could possibly be convicted of a lesser crime but I am told this will not be the case. The Attorney General's decision was that this matter would not go to the Supreme Court (the last court option) and due to double jeopardy Nelson cannot be tried for the same or similar crimes after the conviction is overturned.

I remembered what Brahim told us when we met four years ago. He assured us he would do his best but that at the end of the day we have to respect the system and live within it. I think that as difficult as that is sometimes, it is what makes us different from those who commit crimes. We have not been told when Nelson will go free.

As a final thought I wanted to share that I have at last watched the slide shows so painstakingly created for Brandon's funeral. While looking for possible picture choices for my book, Riley and I viewed (quite emotionally I might add) the very beautiful compilation of photos fit to music. Watching the slide shows was just as hard as I imagined it would be but I was also able to find comfort in the wonderful memories they evoked.

I have small pictures of our family by my bedside. I catch myself glancing at Brandon and feeling unable to truly believe that he is gone. I inhale quickly and then sigh because, for that second, my heart and brain conflict. The logical part of me knows he is gone but the mom part of me cannot seem to accept it when I see him smiling at me in a picture. I exhale slowly and with a lump in my throat, think to myself, I miss you so very much Bran.

www.ingramcontent.com/pod-product-compliance
Lightning Source LLC
Chambersburg PA
CBHW031959040426
42448CB00006B/421